The Jesus Secret

The Hidden Truth

By
AIM OG

A TruBooks Publishing Book

Illustrations Designed by Mustafa Khan-Bey

Library of Congress Control Number: 2005907707

ISBN 0-9760009-2-X

First Printing 2005
Second Printing 2006, revised

Printed in the United States of America.
Distributed by Lightning Source Inc.

Acknowledgement

"I thank Thee, O Father, Lord of heaven and
because Thou hast hid these things from the
prudent, and hast revealed them unto babes.
11:25

Contents

Introduction

The Jesus Secret: The Hidden Truth is a book that finally unlocks the great, historical mystery, which has baffled the world for two millenniums running! Two thousand years ago, such a great mystery was recorded in the life and death of a prophet named Jesus.

The Bible refers to Jesus as a tender plant! However, he began his divine ministry as a humanly sacrificial Holy Seed that transformed into a spiritually righteous rose. The observance of Jesus' crucifixion had him dressed in a scarlet (red) robe, a crown of thorns upon his head, a leafy reed was placed in his right hand, the scars on his back, which botanists refer to as scarification–all these things depicted the botanical characteristics of a seed. And what about when Jesus cried out: "I thirst" and his evil crucifiers felt enough compassion to grant him something to drink? Here they were killing a man, yet concerned that he was thirsty! But this uncanny courtesy only makes sense if Jesus must fulfill the nature of a seed, as every seed needs water!

However, the most compelling, spiritual depiction of Jesus as God's Holy Sacrificial Seed is outlined in the book of Mark: "*And with him they crucified two thieves; the one on his right hand, and the other on his left (15:27).*" Check illustrations on page 110-111. This particular scripture clearly reveals the hidden secret regarding Jesus' crucifixion, as a botanical and spiritual seed because **The Two Thieves** represent **The Two Leaves**! For there is no other reason for Jesus dying adjacent to two thieves other than the fact that the *two thieves* represent the botanical and spiritual *two leaves*.

Christian theologians argue that Jesus died on Friday evening yet he rose or came back to life early Sunday morning. It is mathematically impossible to get three days from Friday evening to early Sunday morning–it's impossible. However, these theologians make the claim that Jesus fulfilled his declaration of coming back to life *on the third day!* In the book, *The Jesus Secret: The Hidden Truth*, it parenthetically proves that this was a major theological blunder.

Thus, what about the second coming of Jesus Christ? The *real* answer will astound you! Christian theology has told us of a resurrected *corpse*, when it was actually about a resurrected *corp*–A CORPORATION OF PEOPLE! Don't waste any more time, read chapter one and I promise that you will be glad that you are an owner of this very fascinating, uncompromising and thought-provoking book!

The Author

The Theology Of *Jesus*

Chapter One

Jesus: The Mystery Name

After an extremely long prayer, the Holy Spirit revealed to me that the name **Jesus** is not just indicative of one person but of many. I said to myself "of many?" So, I went back into prayer and I implored the Holy Spirit to teach me more about this great name Jesus. Then the Holy Spirit illuminated for me a brightly shining cross! However, after my second prayer, I honestly didn't quite see the correlation of the brightly shining cross as a continuation to the meaning of the name Jesus. So, I went back into prayer, a third time, and lo and behold came my answer! The Holy Spirit guided me to take the brightly shining cross "†" which henceforth shall be regarded as my *spiritual key*, and place it in the bosom of this very precious name, Jesus, and there you would get the words Jes † us. While still in prayer, with my face flat on the floor, like Abraham, Moses, and Jesus prayed–I remember saying to myself: "Does this mean that Jesus is Jes us (just us)?" Before I had time to rethink what I had just said–my prayer suddenly ended with the Holy Spirit directing me to open up my Bible and read the first page that I turned to. As I obeyed the Spirit of God, I was led to the fourth chapter in the book of Colossians. So, as I very calmly read this chapter–I came across **a bombshell** in verse 11, it read: "*and Jesus which is called Justus.*" I was spiritually floored when I read this very powerful scripture confirming this very powerful revelation in my prayer.

Colossians 4:11 was a divinely powerful **"411"** – an informational connection in the true meaning of Jesus.

In The Mighty Name Of Jesus

In the annals of theological studies, biblical research asserts the name of *Jesus, which is called Justus*, was first told and last told to the people of Colossae. There is no place else in the Bible where this name is associated with Jesus. However, it has long been reported that the book of Colossians was actually written two thousands years ahead of its time. The book of Colossians is more about *now*, more about *today* and more daily than your *daily newspapers*. Yet, the people of Colossae didn't know what to make of the name 'JUSTUS'—perhaps hitting the **spacebar** between the 'T' and the 'U' would have helped? However, the Holy Spirit was not revealing such a secret at that time. **But Now Is The Time!**

> *"Even the mystery which hath been hid from ages and from generations, but now is made manifest to his saints"– Colossians 1:26.*

Now, it is time for us to know the mystery regarding the *Mighty Name Of Jesus*—as JESUS is not just indicative of a single person, but rather indicative of MANY.

Jesus Bestows His New Name

In the book of Revelation, Jesus talks about giving those, who overcome their life of sin, his **'New Name.'**

Jesus said, "*Him that overcometh will I make a pillar in the temple of my God, and he shall go no more out: and I will write upon him the name of my God, and the name of the city of my God, which is new Jerusalem, which cometh down out of heaven from my God: and I will write upon him my* NEW NAME *(Revelation 3:12).* Colossians 4:11 reveals Jesus' NEW NAME–Jesus' NEW NAME is Jes † us.

Chapter Two

The Truth About The Cross

Theology has duped all of us into believing that this particular image of some character impersonating our Jesus has a brilliant significance on *the cross*. The Bible emphatically speaks against this blasphemous practice in the twentieth chapter in the book of Exodus. Moreover, the book of Psalms has this to say about such abhorrent practice:

"Where is now their God? But our God is in the heavens: He hath done whatsoever He hath pleased. Their idols are SILVER and GOLD, the work of men's hands. They have MOUTHS, but they speak not: EYES have they, but they see not: they have EARS, but they hear not: NOSES have they, but they smell not: they have HANDS, but they handle not: FEET have they, but they walk not: neither speak they through their THROAT. They that make them are like unto them; so is every one that trusteth in them"–Psalms 115:2-8.

The book of Habakkuk scoffs at such carved images as well:

"What profiteth the graven image that the maker thereof hath graven it; the molten image, and a TEACHER OF LIES, that the maker of his work trusteth therein, to make DUMB IDOLS? Woe unto him that saith to the wood, Awake; to the dumb stone, Arise, it shall teach! Behold, it is laid over with GOLD and SILVER, and there is no breath at all in the midst of it"–Habakkuk 2:18-19.

These so-called images of our Jesus are dumb idols and to avoid God's wrath of fury, one better steer clear of these heathen-like practices or suffer the consequences therewith! As Jesus is not to be carved in imagery, for the purpose that *profiteth* a man.

The cross is now a very rich commodity, which has a special niche in the diamond business and very much *profiteth* a man. Jesus was talking about believers carrying their crosses, long before he was ever put upon one and long before the diamond business and long before people started making images of him. The cross doesn't have anything to do with Jesus' image–the cross has everything to do with his NAME. The cross doesn't have any symbolism that he died for our sins–it has everything to do with believing that he came back to life in the power of his NAME (I Cor. 1:18). Therefore, there is nothing wrong with the wearing of crosses because Jesus highly recommended it. However, Jesus told us to carry our crosses, but not to carry our crosses with images of idols and especially idolizing him, or his death. This is blasphemous! **The cross is a divinely powerful "key" and not a divinely powerful "necklace"!** The cross is not for your NECK–the cross is truly for your NAME, which should be spiritually inscribed in the mighty name of JESUS. So, if you are wearing a cross, but not wearing it as a sign of a *key* then you are wearing a cross as a symbol or a sign of blasphemy supporting idolatry–again, this is blasphemous!

Chapter Three

Jesus And The Cross

In the book of Luke, Jesus pointedly says: "*And whosoever doth not bear (uphold) his cross, and come after me, cannot be my disciple (Luke 14:27).*" Indeed, the cross is just that important because the cross is not just a cross but it's a key! Jesus so compelled us to carry such a powerful key called the cross, in order to unlock the great mystery inscribed in his name–JESUS. The cross looks much like the average key, yet it works unlike the average key. This key called the cross is the key to JESUS, but more specifically, it is the key to his name. The key called the cross will unlock the secret *coded* in the mighty name of Jesus. The Holy Scripture says:

> *"Now to him that is of power to establish you according to my gospel, and the preaching of Jesus Christ, according to the revelation of the mystery, which was kept secret since the world began"–Romans 16:25.*

However, Proverbs chapter 3 verse 32 says: "*But his secret is with the righteous!*"

The mystery of Jesus lies right here with us–the righteous! Inherently, we are a people with a morbid predisposition to look for, hope for, and pray for what is already at our fingertips. For over two thousand years, these keys, known as crosses, have been fashionably wrapped around our necks and very much at our fingertips. But, we never knew exactly what to do with them until now. The religious clergy or theologians have given us a whole other explanation of the cross, its real meaning, purpose, and true interpretation. However, the cross was not meant to be revealed before its time. Even Jesus, himself, neither defined the cross as a symbol nor as a spiritual souvenir of his human sacrifice. Jesus only used BREAD as a symbol of his self-predicted, humanly sacrificed body but *never* the cross. The cross had a different interpretation of mighty significance for a latter generation. Jesus knew then what the cross truly represented, but per orders of THE FATHER, he (Jesus) was forbidden to reveal such knowledge for the sake of fulfilling Holy Scriptures. So, the only profound thing or depth of knowledge Jesus ever said about the cross was for a man to "*take up his cross and follow me*" – *Matthew 16:24*.

Chapter Four

Jesus: The Abundant Seed

> *"The hour is come, that the Son of man should be glorified. Verily, verily I say unto you, except a corn of wheat fall into the ground and die, it abideth alone; but if it die, it bringeth forth much fruit"–John 12:23-24.*

The corn of wheat is the fastest growing seed in the world–as a bushel of wheat is produced every nine seconds! One bushel of wheat equals approximately 60 pounds. Sixty (60) pounds of wheat can produce 67 loaves of bread. A modern combine, **a machine that beats out the grain from the husk of the wheat–thereby, promoting its harvest**, can process 1,000 bushels of wheat in an hour. Mathematically, this is 60,000 pounds of wheat in just sixty minutes or 67,000 loaves in just one hour! Therefore, if a family of four were to eat two sandwiches for breakfast, lunch, and dinner, everyday, it will take them 164 years to eat all the sandwiches from the amount of wheat-grain that can be produced in just one hour! In just one hour, enough bushels of wheat can be made to last two generations! That's incredible. Just last year, the state of Texas produced 84 million bushels of wheat, enough to make 5.6 BILLION loaves of bread! Here, you have this one state which has produced enough wheat to feed every man, woman, and child in the world. The corn of wheat is the fastest growing seed in the world, and Jesus likened himself to it! So, now, let us explain the true, spiritual science of the corn of wheat parable using the exegesis of Jesus.

Jesus: The Spiritual Kernel

The wheat kernel is known as the seed from which the wheat plant (bushel) grows. But, did you know that one bushel of wheat contains approximately 1 million individual kernels (seeds)? However, these one million kernels are spiritually regarded as *one million souls.* In other words, Jesus, the original wheat kernel, came to resurrect and save millions of souls.

So, what would you say, was the overall mission of Jesus' divine ministry? It was simply that Jesus was spiritually cloning himself in the form of a spiritual seed. Jesus' mission was to *spiritually* clone himself by the hundreds, the thousands, then millions and then billions or until this entire planet has enough JESUS-SEEDS inhabiting to invoke a global revolution! This is what Jesus meant when he said:

> "*Verily, Verily, I say unto you, except a corn of wheat fall into the ground and die, it abideth alone: but if it die, it bringeth forth much fruit.*"

Therefore, Jesus' ministry was clear as to what he (Jesus) was trying to do which was to spiritually make multiple copies of himself by many multitudes. In principle, this profusion is properly called copious copies of Christ! So, if the world couldn't handle one single JESUS, then imagine having 144,000 of his kind!

In the gospel of Luke, it gives a spiritual depiction of Jesus as this child who will "fall" meaning die, but will be raised again through the spirits of many, it reads:

> *"Behold, this child is set* (predetermined) *for the fall* (death) *and rising again of many in Israel" –Luke 2:34.*

This is spiritually fascinating, in that, we have just read where Jesus said a corn of wheat must fall into the ground in order to produce abundant fruit. Yet in the above text, it very much answers all dissenters, disbelievers, or doubters regarding the person who shall experience such "fall" by making it clear that it is JESUS.

However, there was another very important "jewel" in this very same text, which is spiritually worth mentioning–it depicted that Jesus *"will rise again of many in Israel."* However, you should know that it is not referring to Israel, the state, but rather the spiritual state of those that are or Is-**real** in JESUS. In principle, true theology asserts: "The Is-**real** STATE is not in Israel–The Is-**real** STATE is in YOU!"

Historically, you have always been that "jewel-rē" and through JESUS CHRIST, you will be that "jewel again."

Chapter Five

Jesus: The Sacrificial Seed

Jesus was the Father's sacrificial seed–a seed, which was responsible for reproducing more of its kind. The blood of Jesus symbolizes the nectar of his seed, which represented the pulp or essence, in other words, the Holy Spirit of God. Our Father in heaven desired more dedicated children, like the one HE loved and had in JESUS.

Therefore, the original seed called Jesus had to be sacrificed in order to spiritually reproduce more of its kind. The Father loved JESUS so much that he decided to make the world full of him! So, he (The Father) created and planted his JESUS-SEED within our souls. In so doing, this guaranteed JESUS-ES in abundance, which is really the Father's desire. **Remember, the Father plants in abundance!** The Father doesn't plant just to reap a single product. Therefore, if he sacrificed his Son, through the essence of his Son's seed, then the Father expects abundantly more children of the essence of his Son's kind.

In other words, our Father didn't sacrifice one seed just to bring this same seed back all by himself! This is just theologically wrong and spiritually incorrect. But furthermore, it undermines the Father who we know, operates by his divine principles of abundance. We all love JESUS and our Father loves him more abundantly and this is why the Father sacrificed him as *a seed*–so as to reproduce more of him (Jesus) in abundance. Jesus was blessing, healing, and saving people everywhere he went. Jesus left telling us that:

> *"He that believeth on me, the works that I do shall he do also; and greater works than these shall he do"–John 14:12.*

However, there is no other way to do greater works than JESUS than by being greater in number! We need JESUS-ES in every part of the world and in great numbers in order to be able to abundantly fulfill the Holy Scriptures. And Jesus himself knew this and this was also, why he understood that he had to be sacrificed as the Holy Prototype of his Father's sacrificial seed.

Chapter Six

The Science Of A Seed:
The Botanical Interpretation.

King Solomon was reported as saying: "Go *to the ant, thou sluggard! Consider her ways and be wise" (Proverbs 6:6). But I say*: "Go to the p**lant**, thou sluggard! Consider her ways and be much wiser."

This chapter will deal with the science of a seed wherein we will explore some fundamental, key things in the wonderful and beautiful field of plant life called botany. In the germination of a seed, there are some botanical components, classifications and conditions that must be clearly defined and understood.

<u>The Seven Components of a Seed</u>

1. **The Embryo** is the life-progenitor, which starts the essential life of a seed.

2. **Dormancy** is a state or condition in which the embryo (the life of a seed) is (a) undergoing suspended animation, (b) alive, but not actively growing or developing.

3. **Thin Seed Coat** is a seed that has a covering or shell so thin that water can easily make contact with the embryo thereby activating its metabolism to grow.

4. **Thick Seed Coat** is a seed that has a very thick covering or shell which prevents the necessary water from contacting the embryo–therefore, the seed cannot activate its metabolism to grow.

5. **Scarification** is the process of nicking (slitting or cutting) the thick seed coat in order to initiate the germination process of a seed.

6. **Inhibitors** are antithetic chemicals (enemies) within seeds, which stop the embryo from developing (growing).

   (*a*) <u>Abscisic acids</u>. (the lesser enemies) are very common inhibitors of the embryo, which produce such chemicals in springtime and abundantly throughout the summer.
   (*b*) <u>Phenolic compounds</u>. (the greater enemies) affect those plants that are situated in the desert areas (the hard-to-grow places). This environment causes these plants to produce **more potent toxins** (greater adversities) than its vernal toxins, lesser adversities, called *abscisic acids*. However, these phenolic compounds will keep such seeds dormant until the proper season for germination.

7. **Positive Enzymes** are chemicals within the seed that, when the time is ripe, remove or *leach* away all type of inhibitors–thereby, promoting the seed to grow: HARVEST.

This was an informative but brief little lesson on botanical components of a seed. Spiritually, there is no way possible for a true worshipper of God to fully understand the true significance of Jesus until you first understand him as **a seed.**

Therefore, with the above botanical terminologies under your belt—you are now prepared for our next chapter entitled...

Chapter Seven

The Science Of A Seed:
The Spiritual Interpretation!

1. **The Embryo** is the Spirit of God

2. **Dormancy** is the period in which WE, God's people, will be in spiritual suspension of the knowledge of the mystery until The Comforter comes to teach us all things.

3. **Thick Seed Coat** is the strong but tough body of Jesus.

4. **Scarification** is the stripes on Jesus' back.

5. **Inhibitors** are the enemies of Jesus i.e., the scribes, Pharisees, hypocrites, and more importantly, those who put his body to death.

    (a) *Abscisic acids* (the lesser enemies) were Jesus' mockers, taunters, dissenters, and disbelievers.
    (b) *Phenolic compounds* (the greater enemies) were the actual crucifiers and their evil associates.

6. **The Positive Enzyme** is The Comforter, which will unravel the mystery of the TRUE JESUS as well as reveal all the other spiritual keys that will unlock the mystery of the Kingdom of God.

7. The Harvest is the HEAVEN flowing in the heart, which is actually in the head–thereby it is called HEA(d)VEN.

Chapter Eight

Jesus: By His Stripes We Are Healed

Who was Jesus? Jesus was a divine man of God as well as a divine botanist, who had mastered the beautiful science of botany. Botanical terms which are being used now, Jesus unquestionably knew them two thousand years before they became so scientifically popular. The term in question is referred to as **scarification.** *Scarification* spiritually explains that the stripes on Jesus' back were actually slits or scars made to his seed. Jesus' entire human sacrifice was divinely fulfilling the process and/or development of a seed. The sweet science of scarification asserts that a seed must be INJURED before it can be ENGINEERED. Scarification essentially ignites a seed's botanical engine or potential to grow!

On Calvary, Jesus' terribly torn, brutally beaten, and bloody body was botanically called *scarification,* but biblically called *a crucifixion.* Thus, all of the lashes, stripes, and scars made to Jesus' flesh fulfilled the nature of a seed, which then thrust its engineering (motor to multiply!). So, while people were sadly mourning, this was really the time to be in spiritual elation and celebration–as this was the beginning or early dawn of harvesting multiplied copies of Christ. For, Jesus forewarned us that many would be ridiculing and mocking while others would be lamenting and mourning those pains, injuries and afflictions made to his body. Jesus said to us:

"Verily, Verily, I say unto you that ye shall weep and lament, but the world shall rejoice; and ye shall be sorrowful but your sorrow shall turn to joy" –John 16:20.

The whole scene at Calvary was merely a garden preparing itself to *earth* an abundantly beautiful seed. **There is no way that terrestrial can explain what is celestial.** In the book of Matthew 27:28-29 it reads:

"And they stripped him, and put on him a scarlet (RED) *robe. And when they had platted a crown of THORNS, they put it upon his head, and a REED in his right hand: and they bowed the knee before him, and mocked him, saying, Hail, King of the Jews!"*

As they were making mockery of Jesus, little did they know that they were actually *playing out* a spiritual scene. In the Bible, it points out that human flesh itself represent **grass**:

"All flesh is grass and all the goodliness thereof is as the flower of the field"–Isaiah 40:6.

Therefore, every man and woman present at Calvary symbolized *spiritual grass* and they were spiritually used as a spiritual spectacle, humanly dressed up for the birth of a spiritual seed. These people were actually dancing and participating at a party wherein they really didn't quite discern its music! The evil chanters yelled out: *"If thou be the Son of God, come down from the cross!" (Matthew 24:40).* Again, these evil fools didn't quite understand "spiritual music." The Bible harshly answers them with:

> *"Thou fool! That which thou sowest (killed) is not quickened (cannot come back to life) except it die (be planted in the dirt)"–I Corinthians 15:36.*

Truly, if these evil men had known that they were not actually killing JESUS, but rather proliferating his presence in the world–they would have never crucified him. The Bible puts it in this proper perspective:

> *"But we speak the wisdom of God in a mystery, even the hidden mystery, which God ordained before the world unto our glory: Which none of the princes of this world KNEW: for had they KNOWN it, they would not have crucified the lord of glory"–I Corinthians 2:7-8.*

Had these people known the power, wisdom or truth of what they were doing–they would have given Jesus an over-the-lap, nursery-school spanking and let him go free! Had they known, they would have ordered a centurion of soldiers to protect and see to it that NO MAN KILLS JESUS–but rather wait until he (Jesus) dies naturally of old age. Had these evil men been smart and allowed Jesus to live to be a very old man who died of natural causes–this political gesture would have put a spiritual *monkey wrench* in the Divine Plan of God. They would have actually outsmarted God. But because these people were innately evil to the core, they wanted to be such GODS; they wanted to show Jesus, his followers and the world (for that matter) that they were THE GODS, who had the Omnipotent power of life and death–and they set out to prove such by killing the man, who was said to be God's only begotten Son.

So, in spiritual essence, God said to the crucifiers of that day: "THANKS FOR PLANTING MY SON'S SEED PROPERLY IN THE GROUND BECAUSE NOW I CAN ABUNDANTLY REPRODUCE MORE OF HIS KIND!!!"

The Misconceptions of Theology:

Chapter Nine

About Heaven

Jesus said: "Seek ye first the kingdom of God"–Matthew 6:33.

Jesus declared that **Heaven is first priority!** The kingdom of God is called heaven. Jesus said to seek it first, yet religion has taught us to seek it last (after we are dead). Jesus said that we could have heaven NOW, while we are living; yet religion says we can only *qualify* for heaven–and moreover, it comes after we have perished from the earth. Now, either Jesus is right and religion is wrong, or religion is right and Jesus is wrong. Nay, the former is true! Jesus is correct, and religion is absolutely wrong.

Religion has gotten so bad, that it no longer adheres to its own Bible! Let's take a look at the prohibited verses, which you will **never** hear preached on Saturday or Sunday's traditional church services. In the book of Ecclesiastes it literally mocks this entire theory of heaven-in-the-sky, it reads:

"All go unto one place; all are of the dust, and all turn to dust again. Who knoweth the spirit of man that goeth upward (to heaven), *and the spirit of the beast* (evil people) *that goeth downward to the earth* (to hell)*?"*

"Wherefore I perceive that there is nothing better, than that a man should rejoice in his own works (here on earth); *for*

that is his portion: for who shall bring him to see what shall be after him (after he's dead)?" –*Ecclesiastes 3:20-22*

Indeed, ladies and gentlemen, **your eyes are not playing tricks on you**—for this is clearly in your Bibles! However, I caution you to make several copies of this particular scripture quickly and put them immediately in a safe because, in say, 10, 15 or 25 years—this very same scripture is not going to read this way.

The religious clergy is a severely tight, but secret society of serious scholars who do not tolerate any scripture which poses a formidable threat to the tenure of traditional theology and the longevity of lies, which they have been telling and selling for over two thousand years. So, please make yourself some copies, as a matter of fact, make several copies and urgently put them in a safe for your children's sake. Because after these ill-spirited scholars start hearing that a lot of people are now paying much attention to that particular scripture—they are going to have an urgent *ad hoc* board-meeting and immediately make some changes! This is the ugly side of the people, the principled people backing religion. Yes, religion has a backing, a financial backing—however, this money doesn't come from any of them—this money comes from all of you! You are one of the principled and financial backers of religion yet you don't get any of its pie.

So, again, the Bible is clear, **heaven is not in the sky** and religion has once again told another LIE!

Myths About Heaven

We have so many misconceptions about heaven. But what is heaven? Where is heaven? And how must one qualify for heaven? Well, Jesus said: "*Not every one that saith unto me, lord, lord, shall enter into the kingdom of heaven (Matthew 7:21).*"

Believe it or not, you have some people who truly believe that this is all they have to do to get to heaven. Then there are those who believe that God has this very huge spiritual scale, which has the responsibility of weighing people's sins versus their good deeds. These people believe that Almighty God does a 'who-weighs-the-most' analysis—meaning, if your good deeds outweigh your bad deeds then you get to enter heaven. Then, you have those that believe that the kingdom of God is this GIGANTICALLY HUGE, BUT SPIRITUAL COURT ROOM with flying angels, as the court bailiffs or patrol officers, controlling people from perhaps even shooting God or running out the court room in an attempt to escape a judgment not in their favor. Anyway, these people believe that God has no creative ingenuity of his own, in that, he (God) imitates and adjudicates his judgments in the same way that inferior man adjudicates his. Yeah, these people believe that within this spiritual courtroom, God is going to insert a DVD (downloaded vice disc) and playback everything you've ever done in your life; and God is supposedly going to very occasionally pause this video footage just to ask you "Why did you do this and why did you do that?" And if the court proceeding doesn't go well or in your favor—he (God) is going to push this great, big-old, red button and send you straight to hell. **Yeah right, this is all nonsense!** But, this is how many people in our world think regarding God's Day of Judgment.

Furthermore, its kind of kindergartner to still believe that heaven is cool and hell is hot. Our diplomas and doctorate degrees should really be able to extinguish these flames of foolishness. Yet in too many cases, they just add more fuel to such enormously idiotic fires.

However, don't be discouraged if you are guilty of this same type of wrongful thinking regarding heaven. For, there truly exists a place called heaven and it is beautiful, it is bountiful and it is supremely wonderful, but the best part about it—it's not in the sky. The best part about it is that it is neatly niched within you. The best things in life have always been inside of you and there is nothing outside of you that is greater than what is inside of you. The kingdom of God called heaven is inside of you!

No Fast Running Lines

Although, many of us have been taught that heaven is this pie-in-the-sky when you die—however, none of us are in a rush to test the truth of it. Even the principled advocates of the heaven-in-the-sky indoctrination i.e. bishops, pastors, and ministers of God are in no hurry to test this belief system. You would think that they would want to take the lead in this area and show us how it should be done, or be the first people who will want to make that ultimate quantum leap into the depths of death. However, the opposite is true; when one of them is plagued with a fatal illness—he or she cries out to God to save them from such an indictment of death. But I say no, be not afraid to meet your Maker!

The absolute truth is...they don't really believe in this stuff about heaven-in-the-sky. However, it sounds good from the pulpit or out the microphones and speakers of the church. But don't you get caught out there; don't you be more faithful to a lie that the ministers themselves are flaky about.

Absolutely, no one is enthused; no one is excited, and no one is ecstatic about dying and testing the truism of heaven-in-the-sky. The reason for this is because there is no coming back from death and we know it! Something in our spirits, tell us that something just *ain't* right with this heaven-in-the-sky theory.

We can feel it; we can sense it! At the core of our guts, we are not absolutely certain that this heaven-in-the-sky theory will be able to hold true to its claim. And you know the old saying: "*Always go with your gut.*"

Moreover, how many times has life taught us about "going with the gut"? It seems like every time we have made a critical decision while disregarding our gut feelings—we've paid for it in a devastating way. Thus, if you are attempting to make an important decision against your "gut"—then you are taking the world's worst gamble.

Whenever you disregard your "gut", you increase your chances to experience a devastating "rut". Your gut is the gist of God, which is the essence of God. So, if the very thought of heaven-in-the-sky makes your stomach feel a little uneasy—then that is the essence of God communicating to you by way of his Righteous Spirit, that something is AWRY and it will manifest later as a LIE.

Therefore, go with your gut, as it is God's thermostat, which determines the truth when faced with a lie. Heaven-in-the-sky is such an absolute lie.

The Kingdom of God Is Within

Where is heaven? Jesus wasted no time with explaining the location of the kingdom of God. Jesus plainly taught: "*Neither, shall they say, lo here! Or lo there! For, behold, the kingdom of God is within you*" *(Luke 17:21)*. "Lo" means look or *to look.*

Two thousand years ago, Jesus was teaching people who believed that heaven was some place in the sky, that heaven was not such a place. Thus, Jesus said, as we modernize the language, "Neither, shall we say look here (to the left side of the sky) or look there (to the right side of the sky). For, behold, heaven is within you." Therefore, saints whenever the subject of heaven comes up—please, do not say "lo here, lo there!" Jesus made it plain and simple that we must *lo within*—we must look inside!

In the book of Luke, Jesus taught that heaven is within. However, in the book of Revelation, Jesus preached a more advanced teaching of heaven referred to as the seven churches. In the first chapter of Revelation, you will find Jesus teaching about the earthly churches (Revelation 1:11) and the mystery of the spiritual churches within:

> *"The mystery of the seven stars which thou sawest in my right hand, and the seven golden candlesticks. The seven stars are the angels of the seven churches: and the seven candlesticks, which thou sawest are the seven churches" – Revelation 1:20*

For, there are four important components, or symbolic representations in this particular verse and they are as follow:

1. *Seven stars* represent the angels of God.
2. *Seven candlesticks* represent the seven spiritual enlightments.
3. "*In my right hand*" represents one's righteous walk with God.
4. *Seven churches* represent the seven heavenly bodies.

Church means body of Christ. Therefore, seven churches means seven bodies, but these bodies are all spiritual. In the first book of Corinthians, it reads:

> *"There is a natural body, and there is a spiritual body. There is also celestial bodies, and bodies terrestrial: but the glory of the celestial* (heavenly) *is one, and the glory of the terrestrial* (earthly) *is another"–Corinthians 15:40.*

There in the Bible, it teaches that we have not just ONE BODY, but that we have BODIES; we have bodies in the plural; we have bodies with the "s" at the end. **The human species has many bodies.**

Yet all of these bodies are spiritual and there are only seven of them in number. Some people may have three heavenly bodies but four devilish bodies and others may have five devilish bodies, but only two heavenly bodies. However, in the case of a woman named Mary Magdalene, Jesus had to cast out seven devils (Luke 8:2).

For centuries, we have been taught that there is but one devil, yet the Bible says that there are seven of them. There is one devil for each body within our seven bodies. And our jobs are to cast out all seven of them, in order to reap the ultimate state of heaven!

But, my question is why could not the number of bodies have been eight, nine, or ten? Why did the numerical count of bodies have to be seven? Well, it is because seven is a very powerful number in the kingdom of God. The Bible makes many references to the number seven, i.e., seven souls (Gen. 46:25); seven spirits (Rev. 5:6), seven angels (Rev. 1:20), seven lamps (Rev. 4:5), seven candlesticks (Rev. 2:1), seven stars (Rev. 1:20), seven seals (Rev 5:1), seven vials (Rev 17:1), seven trumpets (Rev 8:2), seven priests (Josh 6:13), seven kings (Rev 17:10), seven plagues (Rev 15:6), seven praises (Psalms 119:164) and the seven sneezes (2 Kings 4:35) etc.

Truly, the number seven is of great significance in God's heavenly kingdom. God has given us these spiritual bodies, so that we may establish a heavenly or godly state on each and every one of those seven spiritual levels.

Heaven is not this place where you go to—heaven is this place where you grow to. Thus, you don't GO to heaven—you GROW to heaven.

Jesus taught about the kingdom of God within, yet the kingdom of God *within* has seven levels occupying seven bodies. Jesus instructed his twelve disciples to start teaching the people the advanced version regarding the kingdom of God. The Bible shows us, more specifically, where the Apostle Paul was teaching such an advanced, kingdom-of-God teaching to the people of Corinth. The Corinthians were learning the dynamic, inner power of the seven celestial and terrestrial bodies within the soul of every human being. Yet, up until that time, this type of teaching was never taught and even two thousand years later—the church is still not teaching its members about these seven celestial and terrestrial bodies within.

The traditional church is so overwhelmed with indoctrinating, its parishioners with this false teaching about a heaven-in-the-sky—a heaven, which is neither corroborated by the Bible nor by Jesus himself.

More importantly, how can you go to such a place called heaven when your bishop or pastor, has yet to explain to you the truth about the seven celestial and terrestrial bodies? You were not taught about these seven bodies within and how the state of heaven must be established on all seven of them. Your bishops and pastors have not learned this spiritual science in their seminary classes. **So, don't expect to hear such teaching in your local church!** The true science of the seven heavenly bodies is the actual and real science of the kingdom of God within! Jesus taught the science of the kingdom of God within and it is not a place that you go to when you die.

Saints, it's imperative that we know that the Father has given us a great piece to the puzzle or mystery of the kingdom of heaven, when he commissioned Jesus to reveal to us that *the kingdom of heaven is within.* When you are pointing in the right direction–you will *aim* in the right direction; you will *focus* in the right direction and you will *be* in the right direction. But when you are pointing at heaven in the wrong direction (up in the sky)–you will *aim* in such a wrong direction; you will *focus* in such a wrong direction, and you will *be* in such a wrong direction.

However, be thankful that the Omnipotent Father made the divine decision to spiritually architect his home called HEAVEN within the hearts and souls of his children. God could not have found a better location to place heaven than that!

Personally, I'm very glad that God didn't make heaven as this place in the sky, because I really don't believe that I would enjoy going there. Imagine being among a group of people all dressed in white, waving at each other, smiling at each other, walking with spiritual sandals, sipping spiritual tea, and having some spiritual conversations about spiritual life in a heavenly stratosphere, up in the sky. Yeah, right! If I had died and was qualified to make it to this type of heaven—**I would waive my rights** and respectfully ask God to send me back to NEW JERSEY!

Heaven will seem boring and very unattractive to me, if it lives up to what the religious clergy have falsely professed it to be. Again, I would not even want to go there—I would much rather spend the rest of my eternal days here on earth.

Therefore, I'm so glad that God has properly informed us that his heavenly address is "**within**" and NOT SOME PLACE IN THE SKY!

Physical Death Disqualifies Life In Heaven

If you physically die, you blew your best and only chance to get to heaven! The God of all the worlds is not the God of this type of heaven. God is simply not the Lord of dead people—I'm sorry, but if you believe that he is—then you couldn't be more terribly in error and far from the truth.

Jesus was compelled to set the record straight on this matter—so, he emphatically put it harshly: "*He* (God) *is not the God of the dead but the God of the living: Ye therefore do greatly err*" (*Mark 12:27*). **The world has greatly erred!** However, Jesus could not have been condemning the theology you are now reading because this book is not indoctrinating that God embraces dead people into his Kingdom.

During the times of Jesus, it was the scribes, Pharisees and hypocrites who were teaching and believing in a heaven after one physically dies. But, Jesus emphatically said to them: "Ye therefore do greatly err."

I know for some, this may be a very hard pill to swallow, as I too would love to, once again, see my loved ones that have passed away but according to Jesus, this is not possible, biblically or scripturally and definitely is not the state of heaven, which he teaches.

Jesus plainly and openly declared unequivocally that heaven is within! So, if heaven is within you, then I want you to explain to me, how can people who have died, be admitted to a heaven which is within the souls of men? Moreover, how can a person that dies, enter into a heaven that is in you? And how can a person that dies, enter and qualify for a heaven, which is in me? If you can explain that, then you are an incredibly absolute GENIUS. In so doing, you would have, also, falsified the righteous laws of God concerning the kingdom of heaven within–this is blasphemous! Jesus said that heaven is not so much as an **inch** away from us, yet religion says that it's approximately a hundred thousand miles away in the sky after we die. Virtually, all of this may prompt you to ask: "So *what is eternal life?*"

The Meaning of Eternity

Jesus said whosoever believeth in him shall not perish, but shall have everlasting life. Once you believe in Jesus you have joined with an everlasting spirit–thus, *"Ye shall never die!"*

For, this planet will "always" have people on it. "Always" means living in eternity and living in eternity means living always. Jesus will never die because people will never die. Individuals will die every day, but people will remain forever.

The Book of Ecclesiastes states: "*One generation passeth away and another cometh but the Earth abideth forever*" *(1:4)*. For the most part, this scripture answers geologists, scientists and a whole lot of church people who believe that the earth will be completely destroyed by God's wrath on the Day of Judgment. But the Bible says that the earth shall abide forever. Therefore, if the earth will abide forever then also, will the human species last forever? This earth will always have earthly organisms on it–and people are the earth's quintessential organisms. And it is only through people that the spirit of Jesus is able to live and last forever–as artifacts, rocks and fossils are unable to do such.

For the most part, we have learned three (3) essential principles regarding eternity and they are as follow:

(1) The earth shall abide forever.

(2) The people-dynamic shall remain forever.

(3) The Spirit of Jesus shall endure forever.

Therefore, Jesus will never die! And this is the true meaning of *eternity* and the everlasting Spirit of Jesus.

Chapter Ten

Virgin Mary: The Immaculate Conception

(Fact or fiction?)

The Immaculate Conception is said to mean that God (the spirit) impregnated Mary without the agency of the semen of man. Yeah right! How dare you accuse God of **spiritual rape!** To commit an act against a person's will is something that the Father in heaven will never do! In all the history of our Father in heaven, HE has never violated the will of man and woman. The human will is the only gift that God vowed to never infringe upon or violate. So, to accuse our Father, in the name of Immaculate Conception, of impregnating Mary is criminally charging the Father with a vicious act of spiritual incest!!! If the Father invaded Mary's body without her consent, then the Father has violated Mary's will—this is properly called rape! How dare these theologians and so-called Bible experts accuse our Father, which is in heaven, with three counts of sexual assault. Our Father in heaven is not a child molester. Our Father in heaven is not a freak; he doesn't have to have spiritual sex with his daughter! How dare you theologians, how dare you fake Bible experts. HOW DARE YOU! This is blasphemous and it is added and compounded blasphemy for those of you who are consenting and riding on this Immaculate Conception bandwagon.

However, some say that Mary was told that she was going to give birth to a child of God. As you can see, somebody else had told Mary of this prophecy. But, I was looking for the more personal statement from God saying: "*Mary, my daughter, you shall have my baby, and his name shall be Jesus!*" Again, this is spiritual incest and this statement still doesn't get Mary's consent. Can the theologians and so-called Bible experts explain how God got around getting Mary's consent? Can they give us a verse in the Bible that spells out how that language was so conversed? Again, how did the Father get Mary's consent? I would like to know. Inquiring minds would like to know. A better question than that is: "Why would the Father want to do this spiritual sex thing with his daughter? Is not the Father all powerful?" Our answer to that is...of course he is. And can he (God) not do all things? Our answer to that is... of course he can. So, the Father didn't need Mary, per se, to produce a perfect Jesus. The Father is very capable of producing a perfect Jesus through the male and female relationship of any couple even through Mary and Joseph. God is just that powerful! And besides why would God fornicate and violate Mary's body like that anyhow, when he knew that Mary had true affections for Joseph? The Bible goes as far as saying that Mary and Joseph were *espoused* (engaged!).

> *"To a virgin espoused to a man whose name was Joseph"– Luke 1:27.*

Why would God violate the body of his daughter just to produce for him a Son? Why would God violate Mary's body, her will and her engaged lover (soon-to-be husband)–Joseph?

Truly, Mary loved Joseph and the Father very well knew this and was very well *aware* of this. I know in the scriptures, it says that our God is a jealous God, but he's not jealous in this type of way and very much not to this horrendous extent. Yet, theologians would like to insult our intelligence and blaspheme our Father at the same time, by accusing our Father to be exactly like that–meaning, he's a child-molesting, jealous Father–religiously charged with three (3) counts of sexual assault:

Count one: 1ST degree Spiritual rape.
Count two: Spiritual incest (sex with his daughter).
Count three: Spiritual fornication (sex out of wedlock).

In the book of John, it reads: "(Jesus) *which were born, not of blood, nor of the will of flesh, nor of the will of man, but of God" (1:13).* Therefore, what makes you a child of God is not your blood, your body, or your flesh, but it is the spirit of God. Two testaments to this fact are in the book of Romans:

> *"They which are the children of the flesh, these are not the children of God"–Romans 9:8*

> *"For as many as are led by the spirit of God, they are the sons (children) of God"–Romans 8:14*

These Bible verses clearly teach us how to be spiritually invited into God's family and how to be regarded, considered, and classified as his children. So, you have to be led by the spirit in order to be a child of God. Jesus was led by the spirit and this is what made him a child of God. So, these two powerful verses are biblical proof that God never intended on making a big issue around Mary being a so called virgin, because John 1:13 clearly makes known that Jesus was not born of blood, the will of flesh, or the will of man, but of the spirit of God. So, it doesn't matter whether Mary was a virgin or not. Mary's virginity didn't make Jesus spiritually consecrated. Jesus' virginity to the Holy Spirit was what made Jesus spiritually consecrated. **Therefore, the femininity of Mary's virginity in divinity is asininity!**

John 1:13 is proof that God didn't need to have spiritual sex with his spiritual daughter to form a physical man as his spiritual Son. John 1:13, maintains and preserves the warmness of a smoking gun in this spiritually forensic science. It unequivocally proves that the entire biblical scene has been changed–thereby, now making it a CRIME SCENE–a spiritually premeditated crime scene. The murdered persons (or people) spiritually killed by all of this were US! And the spiritual detectives, who altered, changed and rearranged the crime scene (script), are the theologians. John 1:13 is that single, thin piece of hair which the sloppy, spiritual detectives left there at the crime scene (in the Bible), which is the DNA (proof) that Jesus' significance is in the spirit, and not in the virginity of Mary (God's daughter).

Furthermore, there is just too much memorializing surrounding Mary's virginity when in all actuality; it was the other Mary (Mary Magdalene) who Jesus said should be memorialized:

> *"Verily, I say unto you, whosesoever this gospel shall be preached throughout the whole world, this also that she* (Mary Magdalene) *hath done shall be spoken of for a MEMORIAL of her"–Mark 14:9.*

Yet, the memorial that has grown to be so popular and so traditionally preached all over the world is Jesus' mother Mary. My question is...how many of us know about Mary Magdalene? You can probably count them on your toes. However, when it comes down to how many of us know about the Virgin Mary—you will need the toes of the world to get your count! So, Jesus made it plain and scripturally clear that only *Mary Magdalene* should be memorialized, not Mary his mother.

Moreover, in the vein of Mary's virginity, traditional theology charges that God is the Father who also becomes the child. I'm sorry, but God is not that desperate to fulfill scripture. God is just not that desperate. As, God could have very easily created a child named Jesus to serve as the brilliant and very perfect example of his righteousness without this alleged impregnation of one of his children (Mary) and so he did. And if God was unable to do so, other than by personally converting his Spirit to the physical form of what we call sperm; if this was God's only way to create a perfect model of his righteousness, then we are all in BIG trouble! What good is a role model if we can't model such role? What good is an excellent role model if it's impossible for us to be like him?

More importantly, how is Jesus serving as this perfect model for all mankind to follow if he is the exclusive product of a single-parent creation—when the rest of us are mere products of God's dual-parent creation? It is biologically, genetically, and physically impossible for all mankind to model a man who is said to be like this. It is impossible for us to be like a single-parent creation and it is incorrect for this type of creation to serve as our example.

An example to us, is to be like we are; an example to us is one that comes into this world like we came into this world; an example to us is if our parents are both creations of the flesh then, likewise, should the parents of the person who is serving as our example, be creations of the flesh. If this is not the case, then this person serves as no perfect example for us.

If Jesus is God's only Son, then who am I? If Jesus is God's only Son, then who are you? This is nonsense! We are all children of The Most High and God didn't need to impregnate our mothers with his "personal sperm" in order to establish us as such. Likewise, God didn't need to personally manipulate Mary's womb with some *invisible, spiritual sperm* to make JESUS. The God of the universe can do all things and could have easily come out with the same **Jesus-product** through both Mary and Joseph—and so truthfully (yet only to the wise) HE did! And if God couldn't do this, then there is no hope for us ever being like JESUS. END OF STORY!

Isaiah's Prophesy

Prophet Isaiah declared: "*Behold, a virgin shall conceive*"—Isaiah 7.14. The book of Isaiah was originally written in the Hebrew language. Yet in the Hebrew language, the word for "virgin" is **`almâh.** Therefore, what prophet Isaiah actually said was: "Behold, an `almâh shall conceive." However, in the Hebrew language, `almâh means *a young woman.* So, what prophet Isaiah really said was that Jesus' mother will be "a young woman," but not implying that she will have this baby without engaging in sex. If the prophet wanted to imply that this woman would conceive without being sexually touched, he would have used a word like *intacta*, which means "*Has not been touched.*" Therefore, all of this simply means that Mary, the mother of Jesus, was a young woman who actually got her sexual oil from Joseph and not from God. So, thank God for Mary and Joseph and for their physically producing Jesus. Mary and Joseph CONCEIVED Jesus as their physical son, yet God RECEIVED him, as his Spiritual Son.

Chapter Eleven

Mary: No Knowledge of Virgin Birth

In the Bible, it talks about Mary and Joseph taking the little boy Jesus to celebrate and commemorate the feast of the Passover in Jerusalem. This was a family tradition that Mary and Joseph participated in every year. According to the Bible, the twelve-year-old boy, Jesus, was more interested in the spiritual matters of theology than engaging in the traditional festivities.

So instead, the young prodigy spent most of his time conversing with the spiritually wise scholars in the temple. These wise scholars were very impressed with the wisdom and understanding that Jesus displayed at such a young age. Particularly, they marveled at how this young kid could open up the holy books of God and proceed to breakdown the most complex details of revelatory scripture.

After Passover came to an end, Mary and Joseph returned home to the city of Nazareth. However, Jesus stayed behind as he continued to peruse, study and extrapolate Holy Scriptures with the wise men. At first, Mary and Joseph were unaware that Jesus stayed in Jerusalem, as they thought he traveled back with the other relatives. Hour after hour, Mary and Joseph grew more anxious, as they realized that they had no idea where their young son could be. They canvassed the neighborhood, checked with relatives, neighbors and friends to see if, in fact, anyone had seen Jesus. However, to Mary and Joseph's dismay, no one has seen the little boy.

Mary and Joseph decided to go back to the city of Jerusalem to make a frantic attempt to find Jesus. After three days, Mary and Joseph finally caught up with him. The twelve year old, Jesus was still in the temple, sitting in the midst of the doctors of theology, both hearing them and asking them questions. The Bible goes on to say: *"And all that heard him were astonished at his understanding and answers. And when they saw him, they were amazed (Luke 2:47, 48)."* Mary and Joseph were amazed to witness the wisdom of little Jesus, but were more amazed and astonished to have finally found him. Although very happy to see her son, she (Mary) was furious that Jesus could think that it would be okay for him to be "missing in action" without their consent. In a very scolding tone, Mary says to Jesus: *"Son, why hast thou thus dealt with us? Behold, thy father and I have sought thee sorrowing."* **Here we have Mary acknowledging Joseph as Jesus' father.** Jesus immediately says to them: *"How is it that ye sought me? wist (knoweth) ye not that I must be about my Father's business?"* And in the following verse it says: *"And they (Mary and Joseph) UNDERSTOOD NOT the saying which he spake unto them."*

Okay, let's carefully examine this biblical text. The Bible says that neither Mary nor Joseph understood what Jesus meant when he said: *"Knoweth ye not that I must be about my Father's business?"*

Particularly, what was the reason why Joseph did not understand this saying, when he supposedly was told about the Father in a dream? But more importantly, what was the reason why Mary did not understand this saying, when she supposedly was told directly about the Father by the angel Gabriel? Were we not taught that the angel Gabriel had pre-informed Mary that she was going to have the Father's child and that this child's name would be Jesus? Were we not taught this? Of course we were. So how is it that the Bible is now revealing, in Luke 2:50, that Mary is puzzled and doesn't understand what Jesus meant by referring to another father? The reason for this was because this was Mary's *first* time hearing about a FATHER of her son (Jesus)–other than Joseph. And, this further proves that Mary and the angel Gabriel NEVER had this pre-emptive, spiritual chit-chat regarding Mary supposedly having God's baby, as the theologians have taught us.

Therefore, Luke 2:50 is proof that what the theologians have taught us was just another **Bold, Fat-Faced, Religious Lie!** Luke 2:50 reveals the testimony of Mary, which exonerates her as a co-conspirator or accessory to the spiritual crime perpetrated by the theologians. This powerful evidence from Mary clearly reveals that *dead people do talk* and the testimony of Mary has told it all!

All of this truly proves that Mary absolutely had no knowledge of a virgin birth allegedly orchestrated by God. Thus, Luke 2:50 further proves that the Infamous Immaculate Conception is a **Famous Maculate Deception!**

Mary and Joseph Did Not Understand

Mary and Joseph did not understand that Jesus, at the tender age of twelve, was already operating in the divine wisdom, which he would share twenty-one years later. At the ripe age of thirty-three, Jesus declared publically what he had privately hinted to Mary and Joseph two decades before. Jesus said: "*CALL NO MAN your father upon the earth: for one is your Father, which is in heaven (Matthew 23:9).*"

So when Jesus said to Mary and Joseph: "*Knoweth ye not that I must be about my Father's business?*"—the theologians argue that this was proof of Jesus acknowledging that he was the product of The Immaculate Conception—as this statement clearly denies Joseph as his father. However, in the book of Matthew, Jesus refutes such claim with: "*CALL NO MAN your father upon the earth: for one is your Father, which is in heaven (Matthew 23:9).*" Here, Jesus did not even want us to categorize our paternal parents with the title "father"—and **Joseph was no exception.** Furthermore, implying that MOM and DAD are acceptable parental titles for us to use. But "Father" is such a great and exclusive title, which should only be used and applied to God.

This all means, that the pope of Rome should not be called *holy father*; and Catholic priests: You Guys Are No Father John's! I heard one catholic priest say: "When I refer to myself as father, I'm not attempting to equate myself to God, the Father. My congregation look up to me as their spiritual father." Well, Mr. Catholic

Priest, God is spiritual and He is also our Father. Therefore he (God) is our spiritual Father!

The Big Three!

The big three principles of Christianity are The Trinity, The Divinity of Jesus and The Virginity of Mary. How could Jesus have failed to talk about the virginity of his mother Mary, when the **virginity dynamic** is essentially a huge part of The Big Three?

Jesus did touch on two of the principles but why didn't he touch on the third–The Immaculate Conception? Why? It was essentially because it would have been an absolute LIE! And, we know that Jesus would never lie to us. Yet, the theologians didn't have any problem telling such a lie because they have been in the business of lying ever since the incorporation of Lie, LLC (Long List of Contradictions) was formed, two thousand years ago!

With all the other spiritual wizardries, Jesus performed on the people–why would he fail to go public that he was the product of a miracle birth called the Immaculate Conception? Undeniably, this would have been Jesus' strongest, *miracle trump!*

I doubt very seriously that Jesus would have failed to add this to his glorious list of miracles. I just do not believe that Jesus would have missed such a grand opportunity. By Jesus publically unmasking himself as the result of an Immaculate Conception, this would have been Jesus' best display of the greatest miracle the world has ever known.

For three and one-half years, Jesus went from the valleys to the mountains, city to city and from uptown to downtown preaching and teaching the Good News called the Gospel and never once did he ever mention anything about a virgin birth. Yet two thousand years later, **it's now the talk of the town!**

It is no wonder the religious clergymen, who concocted the Immaculate Conception theory, had to wait between 300 to 400 years before introducing this new doctrine to the public. These clergymen had to wait until all the people who personally knew Jesus had died. They could never have gotten this Immaculate Conception theory off the ground if Mary was still alive, or if Joseph was still alive, or if James, Joses, Simon and Judas (Jesus' brothers) were still alive. These clergymen could never have gotten this Immaculate Conception concoction off the ground had anyone remained alive who personally knew the intimate details of Jesus' domestic life. They could have never have succeeded with the world's greatest lie called the Infamous Immaculate Conception!

The Virginity of Mary

How can Jesus come into this world, in such a dynamic way, yet fail to mention its dynamics? How can Jesus be the product of a virgin birth, yet fail to talk about the virgin, the nature of her virginity and the reason for her virginity?

The Bible shows that Jesus gave only *one* sermon on the subject of virginity. In the book of Matthew, chapter 25, Jesus talks about **ten virgins!** Now, how is it that Jesus could talk about ten virgins and not talk about the most important virgin, his mother, Mary? If the story of Virgin Mary is true to its claim–well, then, Jesus should have talked about not ten, but *eleven* virgins–meaning, **Mary, his mother, should have been included!** Yet Jesus never talked about the Virgin Mary essentially because Mary, his mother, was not a virgin!

Wouldn't you think that if Jesus were giving a sermon on the topic of the virginity of women, this would have been a great opportunity to segue into the virginity of his mother and the incredible circumstances surrounding his childbirth? Yet Jesus never opted to talk about his mother in this virginity sermon. Perhaps because Jesus did not see where his mother would be relevant to the subject? Or maybe it was because Jesus did not see anything extraordinary about the circumstances of his mother's virginity that he deemed significant or even worth mentioning? However, I find this ironic considering everything we have been taught about Mary, the virgin mother of Jesus.

You would think that somewhere in the discussion of virgins, Jesus would have taken the time out to say: *"Beloved, now that I am on the topic of virgins–I must inform you that my mother was a virgin when she had me!"* Yet Jesus never elaborated on one of the most important human figures in the principles of Christian theology: The Virgin Mary.

It is incredibly unbelievable that Jesus never explained his alleged virgin birth, yet the theologians have an excellent explanation for it! How can the theologians think they have an excellent explanation for a virgin birth that Jesus himself NEVER had an explanation for? Do the theologians know something that Jesus didn't know?

Biblical records prove that both Jesus and Mary knew nothing about a virgin birth. I find this theological striking considering the two are the key people in the, *Jesus: Born of a Virgin Mother* biblical narrative.

Virgin Birth and The Gospel of Jesus

The Gospel means *Good News!* Jesus mission was to deliver and teach us the Gospel–The Good News. So, was The Immaculate Conception part of the Gospel–The Good News?

If Jesus was the product of an Immaculate Conception, and we are suppose to be like him–then, the Immaculate Conception will not be good news–it will actually be bad news! It will be bad news because we will never be able to be like Jesus in that way.

Historically, God has always raised his prophets from among the brethren of the people whom he sought to save–so the people would not have any *excuse* why they could not stand up and claim their salvation. So, if God sends a prophet who is the result of an incredibly miraculous, Immaculate Conception–the people would have an excellent excuse for their shortcomings. The people will say: *"Lord, for surely, Jesus will have no problem being a perfect example of your righteousness considering that he, unlike ourselves, is the result of this amazing Immaculate Conception!"*

Consequently, God would have to postpone his Judgment on these particular people until he (God) sent them an example of his righteousness from amongst them. God has always raised his prophets and messengers from among the people. You cannot send a man, who is part human chromosome and part SUPER-DUPER chromosome from God–then say that he is our example. I don't think so!

Our God is a Just God! God would never adjudicate his Judgment on the souls of people without due process. Yet for God to send a para-phenomenon or superhuman who is the single result of one set of 23 pairs of chromosomes all from a female–and to stipulate that he is our example–will be the world's greatest display of injustice ever recorded from the Most High God, if this were true.

But, God is too intelligent to make the mistake that the theologians are accusing him of. A man born of The Immaculate Conception serves no purpose for God on this earth!

Therefore, God Will Never Make A Man Like This As An Example For A People!

Jesus Never Preached A Virgin Birth

How can you be the subject of a thing yet not address the subject? How is it that Jesus is the subject of a virgin birth yet Jesus never addressed the topic? In the book of John 14:2, Jesus said: "*If it were so, I would have told you!*" If Jesus were the product of an Immaculate Conception–trust me, he would have told us so. The Immaculate Conception topic would have been too important an issue for Jesus to have left untouched. **I repeat: The Immaculate Conception topic would have been too important an issue for Jesus to have left untouched!**

Are the theologians saying that it was not important a topic? How could that be so, when the Trinity, Divinity of Jesus and Virginity of Mary are the three most important principles in Christianity? In the Bible, you can find Jesus talking about the Trinity (The Father, Son and Holy Spirit); and his relationship with Divinity (I and the Father are One). But, nowhere in the Bible do you find Jesus talking about, preaching about, hinting about or even whispering about the virginity of his mother, Mary. Jesus touched on the other two major principles so why not the virginity of Mary?

For three and one-half years, Jesus was on a mission, bedazzling the hearts and minds of the people of his day. Jesus displayed masterful, spiritual wizardries–particularly, walking on water; making the blind see, the lame walk, the deaf hear and raising a man from the dead. Yet the most magnificent feat of them all would have been the amazing Immaculate Conception!

Theologians, if the Immaculate Conception really did happen, wouldn't you think this would be the main topic on Jesus' ministerial agenda? After all, Jesus displayed all the rest of his unparalleled spiritual wizardries—so, why didn't he substantiate the spiritual wizardry of the Immaculate Conception? Why would Jesus fail to mention his never-been-done-before, never-will-be-done-again, incredible and miraculous birth? My question again is why?

Jesus was trying to win souls! Well, Jesus would have quadrupled his soul-winning potentiality had he substantiated his Immaculate Conception. I would also go as far as saying, if Jesus had just mentioned or even suggested that he was the product of an Immaculate Conception, that hint alone, would have quadrupled his membership of followers beyond belief! However, Jesus would never lie or prostitute his spiritual position with God for the sake of more followers. Although, the theologians will do, better yet, have done such a thing as **prostitute the destitute to constitute a religion!**

My proposition to the theologians is please find for me where Jesus preached a single sermon or gave a biblical whisper about an Immaculate Conception and I will personally FedEx you a cashier check for $10,000 overnight! Here is my address:

TruBooks Publishing
c/o Aim Og
P.O. Box 234
Hillside, New Jersey
Zip 07205

Now that you have my address, now give me yours! $10,000 is waiting for you if you can biblically prove that Jesus acknowledged that he was the product of the virgin birth of Mary called The Immaculate Conception.

PS. Please make me an offer to disprove your biblical points for $10,000 and *Watch Me Become Rich!* Then, I would take this money and give it to the poor. **Now That I Have Challenged The Entire Theological World**–let us now move on to our next chapter entitled...

Chapter Twelve

Only Begotten Son

There is only one way that God begets a child and this is through the realm of his Spirit. God spiritually begot Jesus, in a pattern no way different from the way in which he (God) patterned YOU. Meaning, the same spiritual truth, which begot Jesus is the same spiritual truth that begot YOU.

God monitored the birth of Jesus from adolescence to adulthood–so that Jesus would remain consistent with fulfilling God's scripture of a growing seed. Yet, God didn't go as far as awarding Mary with his super, powerful sperm just to make a Son named Jesus. The Bible is very clear in revealing the correct *birthing process* which gave birth to Jesus and such a process had nothing to do with *blood*; it had nothing to do with *flesh*; it had nothing to do with *man*, but everything to do with *the spirit of God* (John 1:13). Previously, we have read in Romans 9:8, which said: "*They which are the children of the flesh, these are NOT the children of God.*" I love how the Bible is so amazingly clear in this area regarding what makes a person a child of God and it is so, not by blood or flesh, but by the spirit (Romans 8:14).

Moreover, the book of James literally explains that God only begets **spiritually** and it is through the word of truth: *"Of His own Will begat He us with THE WORD OF TRUTH!" –1:18.*

The exclusive God exclusively begets not with blood, not with flesh and **not with virgins** but with the word of truth.

Therefore, why are the theologians so hell-bent on establishing Jesus as this only child who is the sole beneficiary of God's magical sperm, when it is clear that the production or the process, which produces the FLESH doesn't have anything to do with making one a child of God? The Bible makes it clear that FLESH doesn't have anything to do with it! So, theologians, there is no need to overwork this theory that Jesus is this special child with this special sperm—especially inseminated by God. Theologians, you don't have to work this hard because the Bible has already proven that this is a lie. Theologians, as children of God, we really don't need you guys to tell us how special Jesus is—for we already know that. And theologians, as children of God, we, also, do not appreciate you guys making our Father out to be some spiritual sex offender in the name of truth using the umbrella of religion.

So, you may ask yourself, why are the theologians so hell-bent on establishing Jesus as the only Son of God, who has not an earthly father? The reason for this was because these ill-spirited theologians knew that we could never fit the bill of being born without an earthly father. Therefore, the theologians said that Jesus was the only man, who was born without an earthly father—thereby forever disqualifying and spoiling any chance of us being like him. Furthermore, how can you model after a man who is the direct descendent of the sperm of God? How can you model after a man who is the superman-child of God? The Bible says that we should be like Christ! Well, this is impossible if this man is made like this. It's impossible for a man/woman creation to act like or be like a man who is a Holy Ghost/woman creation. It's impossible.

However, these ill-spirited theologians did this purposely because they knew that we would keep making excuses, as to why we cannot be like and act like Christ. These theologians knew that if they can be successful in making us make excuses–then we would make excuses all the way to eternity. And they knew that we would never really make any significant inroads in the kingdom of God because we will always be stuck in this type of spiritual traffic. Besides, this whole theory of Jesus being physically born without a physical father just doesn't pass the baby test.

The baby test is the natural intelligence of a child, which Jesus predicated was essential for the entry into the kingdom of God. Jesus said:

> *"Except ye be converted, and become as little children, ye shall not enter into the kingdom of heaven"–Matthew 18:3*

The baby test works like this: If you tell a child that, every human being is born with a mother and father, then later the child hears about a man who was born without a father but only the **MOTHER**–the child's immediate and instinctive intelligence says: *"That's impossible–everybody was born with a mother and* *father.*" The very lustrous baby-test is a child's natural or instinctual reasoning. Instinctual reasoning is a type of reasoning which comes easily and naturally. A child would really have to be *force-fed* to accept that a man was born without a physical father. A child will really have to be *force-fed* to accept such reasoning.

However, a child's first reaction upon hearing about a man born without a physical father is similar to a child's first reaction to inhaling a cigarette: The first puff (inhalation) will produce a cough, which is the child's first warning sign of rejection. The cough signals the child to reject this thing. But, if the child so ignores such warning signs and insists on inhaling (consuming) such a product (doctrine) it will soon be an expert (a pastor!). However, the thing that used to make the child cough, now finds the child immune and unaffected by its effects. The child is so practical with its new techniques now, that he or she can even make smoke-circles, blow O's and ooze them *skillfully* through his or her nose! The child is now an expert on a thing that will exact self-execution.

On John 3:16

In the book of John 3:16, it has Jesus being recorded as saying that he is God's 'only begotten Son'. However, Jesus could not have used such a term 'only begotten' in either the physical or spiritual sense. For instance, let's say that Jesus meant that he was the only begotten Son of God on the spiritual realm. Well, we know this cannot be true because Romans 8:14 says: "*For as many as are led by the spirit of God, they are the sons of*

God." So, the term 'only begotten Son' has biblically failed to prove exclusivity on the spiritual realm.

However, let's say that Jesus meant that he was the only begotten Son on the physical realm. Well, we know that this, also, cannot stand-up to scripture because in the gospel of John chapter 1:13 it says: "(Jesus) *which were born, not of blood, nor of the will of the flesh, nor of the will of man, but of God* (to whom which is Spirit)." So, in both instances and dynamically distinctive realms, the term 'only begotten Son' has failed to establish exclusivity. This really makes one wonder from where came the term 'only begotten Son'.

The answer is a two thousand year old, premeditative cover-up of the truth from a secret society of religious clergymen who were actually enemies of Jesus. Thereby, much of the original doctrines of the gospels of Jesus and his apostles were altered, edited, and re-written by the early church councils during the third and fourth centuries after Jesus' death.

These re-edits of the gospel of Jesus were political *propitiation-adjustments* solely to appease the fiefdoms of the Roman emperors of that day. These Roman emperors, along with their body of religious scholars, translators, and transcribers–formulated the foundation of the Trinity, the divinity of Jesus and the virginity of Mary as the cornerstones of Christianity. Christianity, the name itself, was first introduced at Antioch, an ancient city of Syria and henceforth was declared the official religion of the followers of Jesus. However, throughout Jesus' entire ministry–Jesus never ascribed

Christianity as his religion. Quite frankly, the term 'Christianity' was not even used during Jesus' lifetime, here on this earth.

In either case, these early religious clergymen thought that Jesus should have a 'labeled' religion–so, they gathered together, opted some selections and cast their votes–and presto, came the label Christianity.

Moreover, this prestigious group of clergymen set out to determine which gospels of Jesus, letters of his apostles, letters of Paul, letters of Peter, letters of Timothy, John, and James etc., would qualify as the authentic documents, which would make up the official scriptures of the New Testament for all the world to follow. It was this group of religious officials, authorized by the emperors and kings of their day, who re-arranged, pre-codified, and pre-selected which pages would be included in the Bible. How else can you get a *King James Version* if King James didn't have any involvement?

However, King James was a man who didn't quite agree with the totality of Jesus' teachings–yet, he made himself his own Bible which a third of the planet now has an original copy! Today, we have the King James Version, The New King James Version (as if King James came back and gave us a new one!), The Douay-Rheims Version, The Amplified Bible Version, The Good News Bible Version, Today's English Version, The New English Bible Version, The New American Bible Version, The Living Well Bible Version, The New International Version, The New Jerusalem Bible Version, The Contemporary English Version, we have all these different versions except JESUS' VERSION! Can we get a **Jesus-Version** on this planet? This is a shame!

Although long, this is the extended answer to the question..."*Where did the term 'only begotten Son' come from?*" You can imagine that it had to have come from the various transcribers who had produced various alterations regarding the various translations of the words of Jesus. Therefore, you really have to read through your Bible with a fine-tooth comb because a lot has been MANufactured. But saints, do not get discouraged about the Bible's authenticity because a lot of the important truths are still there—you just have to do a little more spiritual work of unraveling the true pieces to its beautiful puzzle—MYSTERY.

Jesus was the first, spiritual Son fashionably formed by the Holy Spirit of God. The book of Romans correctly puts it this way:

> "*He* (God) *also did predestine to be conformed to the image of his Son, that he might be the firstborn among many brethren*"*—Romans 8:29.*

Two thousand years ago, Jesus was the "firstborn" of many brethren within the spiritual lineage of God. However, the book of Revelation nails this point to the cross:

> "*And from JESUS CHRIST, who is the faithful witness, and the FIRST BEGOTTEN of the* dead"—Revelation *1:5.*

Therefore, John 3:16 should actually read: *For God so loved the world that he gave us his first begotten Son, that whosoever believeth in him shall not parish, but have everlasting life (revised but corrected!).*

This is just spiritually sloppy work on the theologian's part, in that, why would you leave two very important pieces of evidence, which totally contradicts the other? First begotten Son totally contradicts "only" begotten Son and vice versa. First implies that more is coming while "only" denotes that this is impossible! The word **only** is exclusive; the word **first** is inclusive. Only begotten Son makes God prejudice while first begotten Son makes him impartial.

Truly, biblical scripture has proven that Jesus was the first begotten Son of God and not the ONLY. Again, as "first" implies and signifies that more is expected to come thereafter. Well, biblically that has proven to be US!

In closing, anyone who is still quoting John 3:16 in its old, misguided and traditional way *shall* be indicted by the wrath of God for calling him a Spiritual Rapist because that is the only other alternative implication!!!

Footnote

Saints, the way that you can easily determine which scriptures have been "theologically adjusted" is when you come across a scripture, which doesn't corroborate a sister-scripture. For instance, John 3:16 (claims of Jesus as God's only begotten Son) doesn't stand-up to the sister-scriptures, such as John 1:13, Romans 8:14, 9:8 and especially the BOMBSHELL, Revelation 1:5! Saints, when you see these type of inconsistencies it spells a rat–a theological rat at that!

Although, these theologians are extremely astute, scholarly and intelligent men yet their biblical trickeries are falling apart and are unable to stand up to this new forensic science of the Holy Spirit which, by the way, is operating like **Holy Luminol,** as it exposes all the hidden bloodstains in the pages of the Bible where we were spiritually bludgeoned to death. Jesus prophetically predicted that such a great Power called the Holy Spirit will come in these last days to uncover and unravel all the Holy Mysteries. So, woe to today's theologians, as there is no such thing as the PERFECT CRIME. You thought that you could get away with spiritually killing off God's people by fabricating scriptures, but you need to know that there is no such thing as the perfect crime.

Chapter Thirteen

Was Jesus God?

Traditional theology would like to take Jesus out of his Sonship with God! However, Jesus never even made so much as the smallest attempt to remove himself or take himself from being acknowledged as the Son of God. Here are some of Jesus' personal words regarding his demeanor of subordination to the FATHER:

> *"I can of mine own self do nothing: as I hear, I judge: and my judgment is just; because I seek not mine own will, but the will of the Father which hath sent me"–John 5:30.*
>
> *"For my Father is greater than I"–John 14:28.*
>
> *"Abba, Father, all things are possible unto Thee; take away this cup from me: nevertheless, not what I will, but what Thou wilt"–Mark 14:36.*

As we know, Jesus was one of the world's greatest prophetic predictors. And he (Jesus) predicted that the world was going to make him out as this Omnipotent God and liken him to the Father. So, Jesus purposely made all of those statements regarding esteeming and acknowledging the Father as The Greater Authority. Jesus knew that if the world deceivers could make him out as this High, Supreme and very untouchable, Omnipotent God–that many of God's people would immediately go into the automobile business of architecting "*excuse-mobiles*" as to why they couldn't act like or be like, believe like, have faith like, perform miracles like and heal the sick like JESUS. Jesus predicted that this would happen and it did!

In the gospel of John, Jesus said: "*He that believeth on me, the works that I do shall he do also; and greater works than these shall he do*" *John 14:12.*

So, if Jesus was the Father then how could we do greater works than God? My question is how? This is impossible! For the most part, it makes sense that we could do greater works than Jesus because Jesus is our elder brother. However, this scripture makes no sense if Jesus is the Father because we will never be able to do greater works than the Father–I MEAN NEVER!

Jesus was never interested in taking the Father's position yet the theologians were and are! Throughout Jesus' entire ministry, he (Jesus) always acknowledged that there was a much greater power and a much Higher Authority than himself.

God, the Father, was Jesus' Source of Power and Greater Authority. However, the theologians opted to disagree with this by reciting the scripture where Jesus said: "*I and my Father are one*" *(John 10:30).* Jesus made a comparable statement much like the one we have just read, but this time he included US in this glorious mix "*At that day ye shall know that I am in my Father, and ye in me, and I in you*" *(John 14:20).*

However, the theologians didn't bother to take that statement and translate it to mean that "WE" have the same authority, power and position as God, the Father—yet they declared that Jesus had such authority.

Jesus Was Not God

Jesus was not God, The Father! Jesus was divinely commissioned and sent by God to deliver God's message. If Jesus was the Father and the Father was Jesus—then how could the Father have sent himself? Better yet, *why* would he have sent himself? Why would he have sent himself, changed his identity, renamed himself as Jesus and called himself the Son of God, when actually he was both? My question is how can the Father himself have been the Son of himself? This is confusing! God is not the Author of confusion—God is the Author of clarity!

In Business, you have the owner, the office manager, and the employee. Although, they are separate in their respective areas—they still function as this unified team. Spiritually, God is the Owner, Jesus is the Office Manager and you are the Employee. Although the three are separate in their respective areas—they still function as this unified team. Therefore, if the company's stock didn't do well today—the owner says: "**WE** didn't do well today." However, if the company's stocks performed greatly—the owner says: "**OUR** stocks did great today." Whether the stocks performed favorably or unfavorably, the owner unifies himself with the rest of his staff by classifying them as one.

We are one! We are a team, a spiritual team; we work together; we have different roles, different functions, different chores to perform yet we are still part of this same body: TEAM. The Father, Jesus and You are forever ONE!

Chapter Fourteen

Did Jesus Really Die For Our Sins?

How is it that Jesus died for our sins yet we are still considered to be sinning? It doesn't take a whole lot of intelligence to understand that if someone paid for our *sin-bills* then we would be absolved or free from the responsibility to pay such bills. Meaning, when we get to those spiritual cash-registers of God, we should be able to walk pass those pearly cash-registers (gates) without anyone holding us or attempting to hold us accountable for paying for our *sin-bills*, especially when Jesus already took care of this. If we still have the responsibility to come out of our spiritual wallets for payment then somebody didn't take care of our bills.

Paying our bills means to me, the same as it means to you. That is to say—if our *sin-bills* have already been taken care of, per our big brother Jesus, then why should we have to pay again? More importantly, why would we have to pay again when we have the spiritual receipt called remission of sins, which shows that Jesus had already placed these items of sin on his spiritual credit card at Calvary? The point here is... this is incorrect indoctrination and the fact of the matter truly is, WE ARE ALL ACCOUNTABLE FOR OUR OWN SINS!!!

Now let us look at this analogy, as we plunge into this point a little more deeply: suppose you were to take your daughter to the Supermarket and your daughter has gathered a lot of junk foods as her items of choice and, you have agreed to pay for them. Before you are prepared to check out, your daughter takes one of her items and begins walking pass the cashier without making payment. The cashier must do her job–so she stops your daughter from passing by the check out point and then says: "Who's paying for this?" The parent steps in and says: " I'm paying for it–so you can charge it to my card." For all practical purposes, this is the true understanding and simplicity of one person paying someone else's bill, which even a five year old could easily understand. Jesus said:

> "*Except ye be converted, and become as little children, Ye shall not enter into the Kingdom of Heaven"–Matthew 18:13.*

However, you have children in church today, and I was one of them, who do not understand that a man died for their sins yet they still have to come out their spiritual pockets on the Day of Judgment. A child understands that if you have already paid the tab–then he or she is clear and free from making any payment. So, a child takes all of this to mean that he or she can walk by the spiritual cashiers (gates) of God without expecting to make any additional payment for his or her sins! But, as outlandish as this may sound, equally outlandish is the theological doctrine that he (Jesus) died for our sins. Therefore, as long as we are still obligated to monitor our sin-debt, theology needs to stop saying that Jesus died for our sins–just say he died to establish a down payment, **but we must balance the account!**

Therefore, at Calvary, Jesus didn't die for our sins and those stripes, which he took to his back, were for the purpose of **scarification** and fulfilling the nature of a seed. Jesus knew, in spite of his crucifixion, that we still must be accountable for our sins. So, if you are committing adultery then what Jesus sacrificed at Calvary is not going to save you; if you are constantly stealing, robbing and committing burglaries then what Jesus sacrificed at Calvary is not going to save you; if you are constantly bearing false witnesses and constantly telling lies then what Jesus sacrificed at Calvary is not going to save you. And if you unjustly committed a murder, after being saved, then you're going to JAIL and you're going to HELL, as Jesus didn't pay such a bill.

It is the religious clergy, who is responsible for teaching that Jesus died for our sins–however, if that were the case then Jesus would have to immediately come back and die again quickly because we're still sinning. In the words of Jesus: **"Ye have greatly erred!"** It is you and YOU ALONE who must be accountable for your own sins and not Jesus.

In the remuneration of sins, Jesus taught us that there is but one way to pay for our sins, which is something we must immediately do and that is to repent and remit. When you **REPENT** and **REMIT** for all your sins, then *all* your sins shall be forgiven, according to Jesus:

> *"All sins shall be forgiven unto the sons of men, and blasphemies wherewith soever they shall blaspheme. But he that shall blaspheme against the Holy Spirit hath never forgiveness"–Mark 3:28.*

So as long as we do not curse the Holy Spirit then we can pay for our sins. And as long as we repent and do not curse the Holy Spirit, then we shall be forgiven and given by God's grace, all the spiritual money that we need to pay for the debt we've accumulated for our sins.

The two "R–System", called **Repentance /Remission,** is a sanctioned Evil-Exonerator and Sin-Annihilator. This is the type of evangelism Jesus wanted us believers to preach:

> *"And that repentance and remissions of sins should be preached in his name among all nations"–Luke* 24:47.

Let us define these two powerful principles in the Kingdom of God i.e. repentance and remissions. *Repentance* means to have an honestly sincere feeling of sorrow for one's sins to the point of being willing to exact a positive change as recourse (correction). *Remission* means the act of asking and submitting a matter to God in consideration for forgiveness. Therefore, Jesus is saying that if you have an honestly sincere feeling of sorrow for your sins to the point of being willing to exact a positive change as a correction then ASK the Father for forgiveness and he shall forgive you.

So, again, Jesus dying on the cross will not save you, if you do not personally settle your *sin debt* with God. Jesus died FOR US, but not FOR OUR SINS. This is correct indoctrination! We are accountable for the sins that we commit. Jesus died for our liberation, for our freedom, for his love for us, for his love for our Father. I guarantee you that, if you do not repent or personally settle your **sin debt** with God, then I don't care how many times Jesus should come back and die on the cross–yours sins will never be forgiven.

The purpose of Jesus dying was not to die for our sins–the purpose of Jesus dying was to plant God's seed. Besides, you are man, you are a woman–so, be man enough and woman enough to handle (repent for) your own bills (sins). For, this is the very reason why the term "*remission of sins*" is a spiritual ritual in the culture of God's righteousness. *Remission of Sins* is not a "collector item" that is simply there to collect dust. No, it must be used, applied and enforced!

Moreover, Jesus never said nor did he ever imply that he was going to die for our sins. As Jesus already gave us the answers to that dilemma:

> *"The time is fulfilled, and the Kingdom of God is at hand: REPENT YE, and believe the gospel"–Mark 1:15.*

Here is another repentance teaching:

> *"There were present at that season some that told him of the Galileans, whose blood Pilate had mingled with their sacrifices.*
>
> *And Jesus answering said unto them, Suppose ye that these Galileans were sinners above all the Galileans, because they suffered such things?*
>
> *I tell you, Nay: but, except ye REPENT, ye shall all likewise perish.*

> *Or those eighteen, upon whom the tower in Siloam fell, and slew them, think that ye that they were sinners above all men that dwelt in Jerusalem?*
>
> *I tell you, Nay: but, except ye REPENT, ye shall all likewise perish"–Luke 13: 1-5.*

And another repentance teaching:

> *"REPENT; or else I will come unto thee quickly"–Revelations 2:5.*

In the book of Revelation, Jesus was preaching about a woman name Jezebel who called herself a prophetess–however, she convinced and seduced Jesus' followers into believing that it was okay to commit fornication and to eat things sacrificed unto idols. This was what Jesus said he did to her:

> *"And I gave her space to REPENT of her fornication; and she REPENTED NOT. Behold, I will cast her into a bed, and them that commit adultery with her into great tribulations, except they REPENT of their deeds"–Revelations 2:21-22.*

Now mind you, all of what you have read was strictly Jesus' quotes. And time after time after time, Jesus continued to stress the importance of repentance i.e. repent, repent ye, except ye repent, REPENT, REPENT, REPENT. **Therefore, repentance is the only way to be remitted from the guilt of your sins and it has nothing to do with Jesus dying on the cross.** My ultimate question is this: "How did the followers of Jesus receive their forgiveness for their sins before Jesus died on the cross?" Well, you already know the answer, in that, they did **then** what we must do **now**–REPENT!!! God doesn't keep a record of your wrongs because it erases every time you repent. So, repent!

Jesus was wounded

> *"But he was wounded for our transgressions, he was bruised for our iniquities"—Isaiah 53:5.*

This scripture says that, Jesus didn't DIE for our transgressions–he was WOUNDED for our transgressions. **There is a difference!** So, you may ask: "*What is the difference?*" Before we properly align this fine line in scripture, let us first read from the book of Isaiah:

> *"Yet it pleased the LORD to bruise him; He hath put him to grief: when thou shalt make his soul an offering for sin, He shall see his seed, He shall prolong his days, and the pleasure of the LORD shall prosper in his hand."– Isaiah 53:10.*

Now, let us breakdown its true meaning, as we go over this same scripture with commentary in parenthesis:

> *"Yet it pleased the LORD* (God) *to bruise him* (Jesus); *He* (God) *hath put him* (Jesus) *to grief* (By the cross): *when thou shall make his* (son's) *soul* (wounded as) *an offering for sin, he* (God) *shall see his seed* (through us), *He* (Jesus) *shall prolong his days* (as the result of planting his seed) *and the pleasure* (Blessings) *of the LORD shall prosper* (succeed) *in his hand* (at his command)."

This is the spiritual breakdown of Isaiah 53:10! So, the point is Jesus was wounded for our sins. Jesus was wounded for the purpose to scarify his seed but he had to die in order to plant it! **I repeat, Jesus was wounded for the purpose to scarify his seed, but he had to die in order to plant it.** The majority of religious institutions missed this crucial distinction which remains scripturally consistent with the life of Jesus as this Holy, Sacrificial Seed.

Jesus said to his twelve disciples:

"*Except a corn of wheat* (which Jesus referred to as himself) *fall into the ground and DIE, it abideth alone: But if it DIE, It bringeth forth much fruit"–John 12:24.*

This is the ONLY scripture that I know of where Jesus clearly explains the reason for his death. Jesus never said, that he was dying for our sins–Jesus only said that he must die to multiply his seed to produce more fruit. Isaiah 53:5 explains why he was **wounded** but John 12:24 explains why he had to **die.** The point of illuminating this fine line in theology is just to set the death of Jesus STRAIGHT!

If you make so much as a centimeter of a turn in the wrong direction–and keep walking in such wrong direction (believing it) you will soon be miles away from your mark (LOST).

Chapter Fifteen

Jesus: He Rose In Three Days

Jesus' entire life and death were allegorical signs, symbolisms and situations to be understood, as no one knew exactly when he would be born or when he would die. The Bible prophetically declared that Jesus would come without observation! It is profoundly striking that Jesus' *first coming* (physical birth) came without observation and likewise, Jesus' *second coming* will come without observation.

Moreover, the actual death of Jesus is surrounded by so much mystery as well, as it is an extraction of allegory to be interpreted and understood: *He shall die and on the third day, he shall arise again!*

Nearly ninety-nine percent of what Jesus taught had to be interpreted or explained by parables. Jesus was a divine man of God, whose true significance must constantly be interpreted! There is nothing of significance regarding Jesus that doesn't require an extraction worthy of interpretation. Jesus was not meant to be a literal man–so, you cannot take him literally. Jesus was brilliantly meant to be a divine mystery-man–so; you must solve his brilliantly divine mystery. Yet the scripture says: "*But his secret is with the righteous.*"

In the book of Mark, it reads:
"*And King Herod heard of him; (For his name was spread abroad:) and he said, that John the Baptist was risen from*

> *the dead, and therefore mighty works do shew forth themselves in him (Jesus). Others said, that it is ELIAS. And others said, that it is A PROPHET, or as one of the prophets. But when Herod heard thereof, he said. It is JOHN, whom I beheaded: he has risen from the dead"– Mark 6:14-16.*

Back in those biblical times, it was a customary when one saw the same works of a dead man in another person, one would say, **this dead man has risen again!** So, when you see the same works of Jesus in us then you can also say...*Jesus has risen again*, as he continues his great work through us.

Our modern societies have gotten away from using terms, metaphors and figure of speeches, such as "HE HAS RISEN AGAIN" to mean a certain man's spirit has entered and has come alive in another. Therefore, because we no longer use terms like these, when we read them in biblical terms–we don't understand them. The biblical term "*He has risen again*", as we modernize it, means the same person, who has died is the same exact person, who has now risen. Jesus used both terms "*born again*" and "*rise again*" to mean something spiritual and not something in the physical. Jesus said he would die and on the third day *he shall rise again* (Luke 18:33). However, to believe that Jesus meant that he would physically rise again makes as much sense as Nicodemus believing that "*born again*" meant re-entering into one's mother's womb and starting life all over again. Truly, the people of today are suffering from a bad case of Nicodemus-*itis*! And it was no mistake that history wanted to record such a naïve behavior from a very prudent man. As Nicodemus was a very and highly educated man–an intellectual to say the least–yet he still did not know what the spiritual term *"born again"* meant. Likewise, many of us are truly educated, yet we don't know what the spiritual term *"rise again"* means either.

In each case, the terms "BORN AGAIN" and "RISE AGAIN" didn't singularly mean a physical resurrection but they individually meant a spiritual one.

In the gospel of Luke, it chronicles Jesus preaching the term *"rise again"* to his disciples:

> *"For, he shall be delivered unto the Gentiles, and shall be mocked, and spitefully entreated, and spitted on: and they shall scourge* (beat) *him, and put him to death; and the third day he shall RISE AGAIN"–Luke 18:32-33.*

In the very next verse, the gospel of Luke had this to say, regarding the mental keenness of the disciples:

> *"And they understood none of these things and this saying* (rise again) *was hid from them, neither knew they the things which were spoken* (or what Jesus meant by it)"–*Luke 18:34.*

Here, in biblical text, it clearly shows that the term *"rise again"* –meaning, its true interpretation, was even hidden from the disciples! So, if the disciples could not spiritually, mentally, or intellectually discern what Jesus meant by *"rise again"* on the third day–then how is it that THE WHOLE CHRISTIAN WORLD believes that Jesus was talking about three measly twenty-four hour days?

My God, half of the planet has greatly erred! No, this is spiritually, religiously and theologically incorrect! So, you think that Jesus was really talking about *three little days?* So, you believe that those wise disciples of Jesus were spiritually stumped by just 72 hours of interpretation? **Surely, you have greatly erred!** The whole Christian world has been placed in a vicious vacuum of misinterpretation regarding biblical theology. Contemporary theology is to blame for such an egregious episode of evil against the minds of innocent people. However, these very wise disciples were not spiritually stumped by 72 hours of mere interpretation because three days (as we know it) was not the answer!

The spiritual interpretation of three (3) days is one of the mysteries, which is still nicely located in the Bible! Fortunately, these ill-spirited theologians didn't know what to make of it, so they left it alone, it reads:

> *"But, beloved, be not ignorant of this one thing, that one day is with the Lord as a thousand years, and a thousand years as one day"–II Peter 3:8.*

Later, after Jesus' death, the Apostle Peter finally discerned what Jesus actually meant by "*He will die and on the third day he shall rise again.*" A "day" with the Lord is one thousand years–**so, three days mean three thousand years!** The Apostle Peter knew that Jesus' saying "RISE AGAIN IN THREE DAYS" was deeper than a 72-hour analysis and this was why he started the words of the Second Book of Peter, Chapter 3:8 with "*But, beloved, be not ignorant of this one thing.*" You may ask yourself, why did the Apostle Peter preface his words in such a way?

Well, the Apostle Peter predicted that many of us would still be ignorant to this one thing! To worldly people, three days means 72 hours but to spiritual people, three days means three thousand years.

> *"One day is with the Lord as a thousand years, and a thousand years as one day."*

Jesus' entire Ministry was over ninety percent allegorical. Scriptures of the Bible say, that Jesus will rise up again, in the last millennium, which is the last thousandth year before the Holy Armageddon. We have already completed *two days* or two thousand years–now, there is but *one day* or one thousand years left and this is apocalyptically called the millennium. Therefore, Jesus dying and coming back to life in *three days* spiritually means three thousand years, which by the way, is the millennium we are now approaching.

The 3-day Saga Continues

Today's scholars and theologians would like for us to believe that the whole significance of Jesus dying on the cross and rising up three days later was to simply show the magnificent power of Jesus. Wow, as if Jesus had to once again, impress us with his spiritual muscles. Furthermore, rising from the dead after three days was no big splendor of magnificence back in those days, because Jesus had set his own Guinness Book of World Records, when he raised up Lazarus in four days! So, if Jesus wanted to be impressive to the people back then–well, he had to do better than four days! If Jesus wanted to be impressive, he had to break his own record and come back to life in five days! Back to life in five days, is what would have been impressive to the people back then. Besides, Jesus would not have closed his powerful ministry with a physical feat, which was already done and surpassed, as in the case of what he did for a man named Lazarus. No, Jesus intended on closing his very powerful ministry of God with a SPLASH. WITH A SPLASH, was how Jesus intended on closing the chapter of his marvelous ministry. And what a marvelously divine, powerful, and spiritual splash it was and is, when you truly know what he did.

However, to believe that Jesus died and in three days he came back to life—this is purely superficial and shallow. To believe that Jesus died and in 72 hours, he came back to life—this has no true significance or substance! 72 hours is not powerful! 72 hours is not deep!

So, are the theologians saying that Jesus closed the last chapter of his very powerful ministry much like his first chapters? How would you like it, if you saw one of your favorite performers end his incredibly lustrous and extraordinary career doing a show much like the shows of his early days? You would be slightly, if not extremely disappointed! Well, the same is true with God's holy people in Holy Scripture, namely Jesus. We would be highly disappointed if Jesus did all of what he'd done—just for 72 hours of glamour! Jesus already had done the 72-hours miracle thing! Therefore "*the three days*" have to mean something big, something huge, and something that will absolutely blow off the pages of history and subsequently bedazzle and blow the minds of the people of today. So, three days is not big, three days is not huge; three days is not mind-blowing, but Three Thousand Years–Now, That's Mind-Blowing. Three Thousand Years With An Army Of Three Billon JESUSES–Now That's Big, That's Huge, That's Mind-Blowing. That's JESUS! That's The JESUS I Know; That's The JESUS You Know; But More Importantly, That's The JESUS GOD Knows.

Therefore, Jesus would never close the best chapter of his extraordinary career–much like the way he had opened his first! Only 72 hours just to show his spiritual muscles–he'd done that. Making the blind man see–he'd done that. Making the man hear after terminal deafness–he'd done that. Making the lame walk after chronic paralysis–he'd done that. Jesus wouldn't dare close his best chapter much like he had opened his first! But your modern theologian would have you believe that he did. And this is the world's greatest mendacity: LIE.

So, theologians, stop giving us this baby milk interpretation–GIVE US THE MEAT! **We are hungry!** We don't have time to be sipping milk through your religious straws–plus they're CRAZY STRAWS at that. Meaning, they always have you going through a loop–a mental, spiritual, and FINANCIAL LOOP!

Jesus:

The

Resurrected

Theology

Chapter Sixteen

The Seven Signs In The Crucifixion of Jesus

"For he (Jesus) *shall grow up before him as a tender plant, and as a root out of a dry ground"–Isaiah 53:2.*

The 53rd chapter in the book of Isaiah beautifully depicts the life and death of Jesus as a spiritually sacrificial seed. The aforementioned verse you have just read, clearly regards Jesus as **a tender plant**, which will serve as the root, the original, the foundation and the firstborn of many brethren (roses). However, prophet Isaiah prophesized that such *a tender plant* shall come out of a dry ground. The "dry ground" represents the city of Nazareth.

The city of Nazareth was where lived the poor, the beggars, the homeless, the prostitutes, the con men, the burglars, the robbers, the thieves, the downtrodden, and the disenfranchised. It was a slum or ghetto city, which was barren of great talents, skills, education and intelligence. Thus, came the saying: "*Can there any good thing come out of Nazareth? (John 1:46).*" Jesus was that Nazarene that came out of Nazareth. Nazareth was that biblically dilapidated "dry ground" from which *that good thing* called Jesus had emerged.

In this chapter, we will define, interpret and graphically display the seven signs of this especially important Nazarene named Jesus with artistic comparisons regarding the biblical principle of his crucifixion:

1. *The Cross* (The key to the mighty name JESUS).

2. .*Jesus' Body* (The Seed).

3. *The Stripes* (Scarification).

4. *He Thirst* (The vinegar represents the **water**–John 19:28-29).

5. *Crown of Thorns* (The blossoming of a seed–Mark 15:17).

6. *The Two Thieves* (represent the two leaves–Mark 15:27).

7. *The Third Day* (A day is with the Lord as a thousand years–II Peter 3:8).

Figure 1.1

Biblical Representation:

"***The Cross***"

"...Take up his cross and follow me."–Matthew 16:24

Figure 1.2

Spiritual Translation:

"*The Key*"

"*...And Jesus which is called Justus.*"–Col 4:11

Figure 2.1

Biblical Representation:

"Jesus' Body"

" *A sacrificed human-seed.*"

Figure 2.2

Spiritual Translation:

"***The Seed***"

"...He shall see his seed."
–Isaiah 53:10

Figure 3.1

Biblical Representation:

"The Stripes"

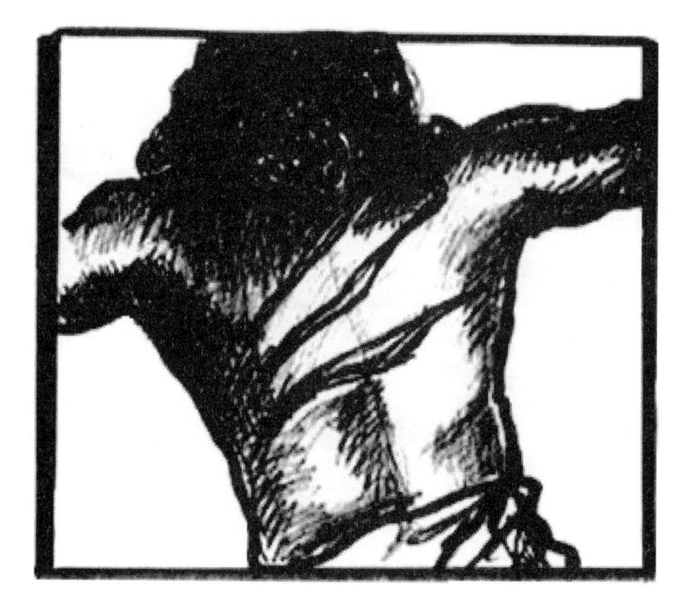

"...And with his stripes we are healed."–Isaiah 53:5

Figure 3.2

Spiritual Translation:

"***Scarification***"

"A seed must be **injured** before
it can be **engineered**."

Figure 4.1

Biblical Representation:

"He Thirst"

"I thirst."–John 19:28

Figure 4.2

Spiritual Translation:

"Vinegar, which represent the water"

"A seed needs water in order to grow"

Figure 5.1

Biblical Representation:

"Crown of Thorns"

"Platted a crown of thorns, and put it about his head." –Mk 15:17

Figure 5.2

Spiritual Translation:

"*Sprouting as a Seed*"

Jesus' head is the bud of a rose wrapped with a thorny stem.

Figure 6.1

Biblical Representation:

"***The Two Thieves***"

"And with him they crucified two thieves; the one on his right hand, and the other on his left." –Mark 15:27

Figure 6.2

Spiritual Translation:

"*The Two Leaves*"

Jesus, the tender plant with two leaves: "And the scripture was fulfilled, which saith, and he was numbered (counted) with the transgressors (Mark 15:28)." The divine number is 3.

Figure 7.1

Biblical Representation:

The Third Day

"And the third day he shall rise again."—Luke 18:33

Figure 7.2

Spiritual Translation:

3,000 YEARS!

"One day is with the Lord as a thousand years."–II Peter 3:8

DISCLAIMER: These images are not actual depictions of Jesus, rather are mere illustrations to the explicit and prolific depictions, which already exist in modern, religious clericalism.

Chapter Seventeen

Jesus: Til The Comforter Comes

In the words of Jesus: "*But when the Comforter is come, whom I will send unto you from the Father, even the Spirit of truth, which proceedeth from the Father, he shall testify of me*"–*John 15:26.*

Jesus asserted that the purpose for the coming of the Comforter is: "*He shall teach you all things*" (*John 14:26*). My question is..."*All of what?*"

The Christians of today know no more than the early Christians of two thousand years ago. Christians today believe that "*Jesus was the only begotten Son of God*"– well, two thousand years ago, they believed this too. Christians today believe that "*By his stripes we are healed*"– well, two thousand years ago, they believed this too. Christians today, also, believe that "*Jesus died and on the third day, he rose from the dead*"–and two thousand years ago, they believed that too. All of the Christian principles so taught today were the same identical principles, which were taught back then or two thousand years ago. So, it's quite clear that Christians today have not been taught anything NEW. I'm still waiting for something that is new, something, which is fresh, something that was once a MYSTERY.

Jesus said that the Comforter would teach us all things. When Jesus said that the Comforter will teach us all things–this meant "everything"; this meant the Comforter would not pull any punches; this meant that the Comforter would hold nothing back; this meant that the Comforter would finally unlock the two thousand year old mystery. So, I fail to understand what is all this talk about Jesus returning any day now! How is that so, when Christians have not been taught "all things"? If there is just one biblical fact, it is knowing that Jesus can and will only come after the Comforter has done its job of teaching us "all things". For, this is the biblical priority regarding the scriptures of the coming of JESUS. Jesus said: "*This generation shall not pass, til all these things be done (Mark 13:30).*" So, has anyone talked to the Comforter; and has anyone heard from the Comforter; and does anyone actually know who and what the Comforter is–and where, when, and how the Comforter is suppose to come? **Well, there will be no second coming of Christ til first cometh the Comforter.** So, until that happens, we are just being hoodwinked (deceived). Somebody has told us that this spiritual cake is well done–when actually the batter is still *liquidy!*

Inference

All over the world, Christians are hearing the same exact things (doctrines) but just under different sound systems (churches).

So, saints until you start hearing new doctrines or teachings which are unlocking these biblical truths, codes, mysteries and teachings of Jesus, then Jesus himself is delayed and far from making an arrival.

Chapter Eighteen

The Comforter

"It is expedient for you that I go away; for if I go not away, the Comforter will not come unto you"–John 16:7.

First and foremost, we have learned that Jesus' body was a sacrificial Holy Seed. Secondly, if such *seed* is visible then this means that it has not been *planted* and it further means that it is not preparing itself to grow for the purpose of reaping a harvest! So, this is what Jesus meant by: *"If I go not away, the Comforter will not come."* The Comforter is the ENZYME, which is embedded inside Jesus' seed. Therefore, you have to be a Jesus seed to receive such power from the Comforter.

The Power

The first Comforter taught us some of the mysteries, which gave us some use of the Holy Power. However, Jesus said that the Father shall give us 'another Comforter', which will teach us all things and which will make available for us, all the power of the Holy Spirit:

"But the Comforter, which is the Holy Ghost, whom the Father will send in my name, he shall teach you all things and bring all things to your remembrance, whatsoever I have said unto you"–John 14:26.

But the best part of this scripture was when Jesus said that the Father shall send such Comforter in the name of Jesus, which means Jes † us. However, what really blew my mind was when I discovered the true meaning of the Comforter. In the original writing of the Hebrew language, the word for Comforter is nâcham, which means *comfort one's self!* **The "self" is "one" with the Comforter–as you and the Comforter are one.** Therefore, we must comfort ourselves with the Comforter. The Comforter is the Holy Spirit.

Right now, the spirit of the Comforter is spreading like a righteous virus! Many people are catching this Holy Righteous Flu because it is spreading like a wildfire. But it's not making people sick; on the contrary, it's making them healthy (whole). Pray to God that he comforts you with the Comforter when he comes and he is coming! For many, the Comforter has already come, but pray to God that he comes to you.

Another Comforter

The annals of biblical history have the Pharisees asking Jesus for a 'sign', regarding the heavenly things which he was teaching concerning the mysteries of the kingdom. But Jesus replied: *"There shall no sign be given unto this generation" (Mark 8:12).* Indeed, those were pretty harsh words coming from Jesus but as Jesus would say: *"Nevertheless, I tell you the truth!"*

Now, to our title of this section: **Another Comforter**. In the book of John, Jesus was reported as saying, that he will pray to the Father for "another Comforter" to come to us and one which will abide with us forever (14:16). Therefore, if Jesus prayed that "another Comforter" would come then we must have had a "previous Comforter". What was the "previous Comforter"? What was the job or duty of the "previous Comforter" and what did it actually do? These are very good questions, regarding the "previous Comforter", which require very good answers.

Firstly, what is the Comforter? In the gospel of John 14:26, Jesus taught that the Comforter is the Holy Spirit! In the first book of Corinthians, it reads:

> *"As it is written the first man Adam was made a living soul; the last Adam was made a quickening spirit"–I Corinthians 15:45.*

The spiritual interpretation is: the "previous Comforter" made man, a living soul, but "another Comforter" will come to make man, a quickening spirit! In the same chapter but verse 47 it reads: "*the first man is the earth, earthy: the second man is the Lord from heaven.*" The first thing that must be clarified is that the 'first man' and 'second man' are both the same person–just like the 'first Comforter' and 'second Comforter' are both the same Holy Power. The purpose of the 'first Comforter' was to help to condition the 'first man' in his early stages of human development, yet, the sole purpose of the 'second Comforter' is to condition the 'second man' (the inner man) to attain the highest level or fullness of his spiritual development in the image and likeness of his Father (God).

> *"And as we have borne the image of the earthly, we shall also bear the image of the heavenly"–I Corinthians 15:49.*

Furthermore, you will notice an interesting trinity in biblical theology:

1. There is a 'first man' and a 'second man'.
2. There is a 'first Comforter' and a 'second Comforter'.
3. There is a 'first Jesus' and the coming of a 'second Jesus'.

In the Bible, Jesus talks about some of the things, which we should expect from the Holy Spirit, the Comforter, when it comes:

> *"I have yet many thing to say unto you, but ye cannot bear them now. Howbeit when he, the Spirit of truth* (the Comforter), *is come, he will guide you into all truth: for, he shall not speak of himself; but whatsoever he shall hear, that shall he speak: and he will shew you things to come"–John 16:12,13.*

> *"But God hath revealed them* (the mysteries) *unto us by his spirit: for the spirit searcheth all things, yea, the deep thing of God"–I Corinthians 2:10.*

> *"But this spake he of the spirit, which they believe on him should receive: for the Holy Spirit was not yet GIVEN: because THAT JESUS was not yet glorified"–John 7:39.*

Whoa! That's an incredible bombshell!!! What does the Bible mean by "For the Holy Spirit was not yet given, because 'THAT JESUS' was not yet glorified"? Who is "THAT JESUS"? What is "THAT JESUS"? Where is "THAT JESUS"? This all tells us that "another Comforter" was for the purpose of "another generation" to serve "another Jesus" who is scripturally called

"THAT JESUS". "THAT JESUS" will be taught all of God's hidden mysteries in the kingdom of heaven. We will be explaining more about "THAT JESUS" in our forthcoming chapter entitled *"Jesus: The Second Coming."* But until then, we would like for you to spiritually digest our next chapter entitled...

Chapter Nineteen

Jesus: Cometh In Another Form

"He (Jesus) *appeared in another form*"–*Mark 16:12.*

The Bible testifies that Jesus appeared "IN ANOTHER FORM." This could not have been talking about Jesus appearing as a spook or spirit because a spirit has no form! Therefore, for Jesus to appear *in another form* meant that Jesus manifested not in the same physical form or with the same body, hands, face, and feet which everyone who knew him was familiar with. But, rather, he (Jesus) appeared in a form that none of these people were familiar with–which was through some other form called "another form"–biblically, this is referring to US! However, the theologians will have you believe that the reason why the disciples didn't recognize Jesus at first was because, after viewing Jesus' badly beaten body on the cross, they (disciples) didn't recognize him all healed and cleaned up. Yeah right, as if they didn't know how Jesus looked prior to being led to the cross. These religious scholars work hard to keep you trapped in spiritual death. And these people are extremely gutsy and have the audacity to insult our intelligence with such superficial, shallow interpretation of God's Holy Scriptures.

Still today, especially during Easter, there is this big thing about whether or not Jesus actually came back to life in three days. Nearly, half the planet is saying he (Jesus) came back to life in three days and the other half (either don't know or) is saying that he didn't. But in either case, it doesn't even matter because the true meaning is purely spiritual! For, Jesus used the interpretation of three days as a "sign" for another generation. Jesus defined "a day" like the second book of Peter 3:8 defines "a day": *One day is with the Lord as a thousand years.* Therefore, I don't care about how your theologian defines "a day", or how your bishop defines "a day", or how your pastor defines "a day"—I'm spiritually on the side of the Lord regarding how he defines "a day". So, it really doesn't matter what any side or all sides are saying **because they are all spiritually wrong!**

People of God, we have to stop drinking warm milk and start eating hot food (meat and potatoes!). For those of us who discern the spiritually deep things of the spirit—we're *lactose-intolerant.* But, for those of us who do not—are very *tolerant for lactose* (intrigued by the insignificant interpretation of scripture).

Jesus came in another form and this other form is just <u>US</u>!

Chapter Twenty

Jesus: Will We See Him Again?

Jesus said to his disciples that he would leave them and they (meaning WE) would see him no more. *"Because I go to my Father, and ye see me no more"–John 16:10.* Two thousand years ago, the definition of "no more" meant never again. And even to this day or two thousand years later, the definition for "no more" still means never again. **We Will Not See Jesus Ever Again <u>In His Same Flesh</u>!**

However, the Bible explicitly tells us later that the disciples did actually witness Jesus again, but there was something very strange about this "second encounter". After the resurrection, the Bible tells us that, when Jesus first approached his disciples, they didn't **recognize** him (John 20:14; Luke 24:15-31).

Another text discloses that Jesus had to jog their **remembrance** of him (Matthew 28:17). But another striking text reveals that one of his disciples just flat out and blatantly **doubted** it was him (John 20:25). However, after **careful examination**, the disciples concluded that this *Jesus figure* was the real Jesus (John 20:20).

There are great number of mysteries, in all these biblical narratives. Yet, they all have spiritual significances that must be comprehensibly interpreted. First and foremost, all these narratives are allegorical! If these narratives were not meant to be allegorical then this means that Jesus told a lie because the disciples did see him again. Therefore, these narratives were for spiritual purposes and discernments only!

Now, let us pursue the spiritual discernments regarding this very important lesson of Jesus' resurrection:

1. *When Jesus first approached his disciples, they didn't recognize him as Jesus.*
The spiritual discernment: When Jesus' *"two thousand years later"* disciples become introduced to the true understanding of Jesus–they are not going to recognize and accept it as the real Jesus either.

2. *The disciple, known as doubting Thomas, doubted that Jesus was indeed resurrected or had come back to life.*
The spiritual discernment: Jesus' *"two thousand years later"* disciples will be saturated with millions of **doubting-Thomas'** who will also doubt that Jesus will be resurrected or coming back to life, through the spirits of people.

3. *The Bible reveals where Jesus had to invoke their remembrance of him.*
The spiritual discernment: Jesus' *"two thousand years later"* disciples are going to need the Comforter to invoke their remembrance of Jesus' teachings:

> *"But the Comforter which is the Holy Ghost, whom the Father will send in my name, he will teach you all things,*

and bring all things to your REMEMBRANCE, *whatsoever I have said unto you"–John 14:26.*

4. After careful examination, Jesus' disciples concluded that this Jesus figure was indeed a resurrected Jesus.
The spiritual discernment: After searching the scriptures and ascertaining the REAL TRUTH–Jesus' "*two thousand years later*" disciples are, likewise, going to conclude that the man who died at Calvary is now personifying the brethren–God's people. Therefore, it is biblically proven that we will see Jesus again–this Jesus is JUST US!

Chapter Twenty-One

Jesus: Cometh Through His Name

All throughout the New Testament, Jesus repeatedly made many references to his name:

[1] In my name–Mark 16:17.
[2] Ask the Father in my name–John 15:16.
[3] Drink in my name–Mark 9:41.
[4] Believe in the name–John 3:18.
[5] Bear my name–Acts 9:15
[6] Gathered together in my name–Matthew 18:20.
[7] For many shall come in my name–Luke 21:8.
[8] At that day ye shall ask in my name–John 16:26.
[9] I will write upon him my new name–Revelation 3:12.
[10] Thou holdest fast my name–Revelation 2:13.

Truly, we have to hold fast to Jesus' name, and bear (carry) his name because within his name is also, our name.

The second coming of Christ will come about in the power of the brethren. The resurrection of Jesus Christ will come about in the power of his own name. Thus, every time Jesus said to us, IN MY NAME, he (Jesus) was talking about US.

We, the people of God, are the only people who are in Jesus' name. Jesus loved us so much that he put us in his bosom–the bosom of his NAME. For, there is no greater love than that!

The scripture says, Jesus, which is called JUSTUS. *Jesus* is just us and *Jes us* is Jes † us:

I am Malcolm X,
I am Malcolm X,
I am Malcolm X.

No, I AM JESUS!

Chapter Twenty-Two

Jesus: The Second Coming

In the gospel of Luke 18:34 it says, Jesus' true identity was regarded as a secret and we are not talking about Jesus' first coming–we're talking about Jesus' second coming. That's the real secret! Therefore, such **a great secret** can't be the same old information that every new member gets when he or she first joins a church and wants to learn about Christ. That can't be the secret! For there are over a billion Christians and some researchers even say that the Christian world population is growing and approaching nearly two billion people. Quite frankly, I have never heard of something being regarded as a secret, when nearly two billion people already know what it is. That's not a secret–that's mass media! THAT'S A PUBLIC ANNOUNCEMENT!

However, scripture says, that the Son of man's true identity will come without observation.

First cometh the 144,000!

> "*And they sung* (spoke the truth of the mysteries) *as it were a new song* (a new revelation) *before the throne* (the kings, presidents, governors) *and before the four beast, and the elders: and no man could learn* (understand) *that song* (called 'That Jesus') *but the hundred and forty and four thousand* (144,000), *which were redeemed* (spiritually resurrected) *FROM THE EARTH. These*

were redeemed from among men, being the first fruits unto God and to the lamb (Jesus)"–*Revelations 14:3-4.*

The 144,000 first fruits of God are on this planet right NOW! However, they are not organized in any particular group, gathering or organizational structure which is physical–they are scattered out in a group, gathering, or organizational structure which is purely spiritual yet in human form.

Truly, no one really knows whether he or she is qualified to be one of the 144,000 first fruits of God's great harvest. However, we must spiritually strive hard to become a member of this special, elite, and divine group–by living morally upright–as only God can choose who will be accepted and selected into this spiritually illustrious group. Truly, there are great benefits in being or becoming one of the "firstborns". To be a "firstborn" means that the heavens will avail you with first dibs! To have first dibs in a beautifully rich and abundant kingdom is a very good thing.

Moreover, being one of the chosen "firstborns" has nothing to do with a "when-you-got-saved" enrollment log. A "firstborn" membership has nothing to do with the day, month or year, you were saved nor does it heavenly concern itself with prioritizing members of the church, temple, or synagogues with special privileges just because they were saved before you were.

Truly, those things do not count or constitute membership in the world of the "firstborns". What constitutes membership in the fold or family of the firstborn is not who got saved first, but rather who sought the kingdom of God first—and found it! This is the primary pathway to becoming a member of this very special group of people called the "firstborns". Jesus had this to say regarding those who are spiritually auditioning to become members of this especially unique group: "*For many are called, but few are chosen"–Matthew 22:14*. Overall, becoming a "firstborn" means that you will get your heavenly benefits NOW while everyone else will get their benefits LATER. Now, to....

That Jesus

Who is "That Jesus"? What is "That Jesus"? Where is "That Jesus"? You are "That Jesus" which the Bible has been talking about and will come in these last days. Jesus knew that his seed must be sacrificed so that it could spiritually germinate and abundantly produce more of its kind. Therefore, if the world couldn't handle one single Jesus then imagine having to deal with 144,000 of his kind? The Day of Judgment is the day of too many Jesus-es! This is the real Day of Judgment that frightens the wicked people of this world.

Do you know or have any idea how much saving, healing, and miracle-performances that can come from 144,000 Jesus-es parading this entire planet? As one single apple seed will produce enough apples to feed an entire family. But just one Jesus seed shall produce enough Jesus-es to save and feed the entire world.

The second coming of Christ will come about in the power of the brethren. Church means body of Christ. As no man can ever go to church—everyman must be a church. We are the church of God; we are the body of Christ, which is coming in these last days. We are "That Jesus". However, let us not be afraid to know that we are the embodiment of this man named Jesus, biblically referred to as "That Jesus", who will be responsible for coming in the last days to destroy the world of Satan. Jesus prophesied about the *Jesus in us* which will be coming in the last days to massively destroy the wicked foundation of this evil world of sin. Jesus is truly counting on us and the count of our number is 144,000! Thereby, from the original seed (Jesus), we have nearly two billion people who now have come to love him. Frankly, this all means that if one (1) seed can bring nearly two billion people to love him, then 144,000 Jesus-seeds should suffice the entire planet!

Jesus was a sacrificial seed and a seed does nothing but send the essence of itself though such productive power of its organic fruit. **We are Jesus' spiritually organic fruit!**

Biblically, this is what Jesus meant by:

> "*It is expedient* (to your advantage) *for you that I* (the original seed) *go away* (make my sacrifice to the soil for souls); *for if I go not away* (or choose not to make my sacrifice to the soil for the sake of souls), *the Comforter* (the power of God) *will not come unto you; but if I depart* (make my sacrifice to the soil for souls), *I will send* (bring forth) *him* (the power of God) *unto you* (us)."

Yes, this is the true interpretation of John 16:7 and also is the fulfillment of "That Jesus"!

Chapter Twenty-Three

Jesus Has Arrived!

Jesus didn't die; Jesus transformed! Jesus transformed into a seed so that he could perform at a much greater capacity and service more people to bring about greater communities. *Jesus has arrived!* Jesus is here! Jesus is Jes us! It's not going to be an individual Jesus that will come and save us–it's going to require a multitude of Jesus-es to come and save us. We're going to need a lot of Jes us or Jesus-es to bring us out of our present conditions. Therefore, Christ is not meant to be one, but a community of many. Jesus is Just Us!

We are Jesus' best chance of making a second coming. And we are Jesus' only chance of coming back to save the world. This is what the Bible meant when it said: "*He will come without observation.*" However, this is referring to US. For that to be possible, the Bible has to be referring to US because we are already situated in this world. So, if we are the ones to come no one will ever suspect it! For us to come will make biblical and scriptural sense. For us to come will truly catch everyone off guard. Besides, who in their right mind, pardon me, I mean wrong mind, will ever think that YOU will be part of this coming? No one will ever suspect YOU; no one will ever suspect God's children; no one will ever suspect "just us"–the scripturally promised and new and improved JESUS.

Truly, if we are to come, we will catch the entire world by surprise–therefore, this is exactly why God is sending us—so, that we may catch the world by surprise. There is no better or a more divine plan to destroy an enemy than by using your spiritual soldiers which are already deployed in the enemy's camp. An internal revolt is an enemy's worst NIGHTMARE! Therefore, the time has come for God's children to put the enemy to eternal death for the sake of good by the shining sword of righteousness.

However, don't faint for a minute! Don't think that just because you are coming, as a member of this body called THE SECOND COMING OF CHRIST—that this, in any way, will lessen the effects of the resurrection! Don't make that mistake! Jesus spoke highly of YOU and prophesied about the mighty wonders and powers that YOU possess. Two thousand years ago, Jesus openly declared to the world that when the Holy Power called "another Comforter" comes to us—that the works that he did, we shall do but we shall do greater than all the works, he did (John 14:12).

Therefore, the Father, in heaven, will not have permitted Jesus to make mockery of himself by making a public statement like that—if Jesus himself had to still "stick-up" for us at the end of the day called the final Day of Judgment. Our Father, in heaven, would have never allowed Jesus to boast about our powers like that and then have Jesus come back on the planet two thousand years later, in order to finalize our final war against Satan. For, Jesus already defeated Satan—well then, we must defeat him too! Mr. Satan has over a billion soldiers—well, Sir Jesus has over a billion too!

The devil is the name of a man yet Satan is the name of his spirit!

Truly, this is our fight and we must fight it! We must fight and defeat Satan using the same spiritual methods and tactics that our big brother Jesus displayed, two thousand years ago. Jesus was the victor then and we must be such victors NOW. **Remember, Satan's kids cannot defeat God's kids.** We are God's kids and I'm not kidding! The Father, in heaven, spiritually prepared, trained and conditioned Jesus to win his battle against Satan. The scriptures of God are designed to show us how to win. The New Testament, in particular, gives us the spiritual system, program and regimen that the Father had given to Jesus, and which had made Jesus such a success against his open enemy–Satan. The Father has this same spiritual system of success for US–but only if we follow it, in the same manner, as illustrated by his first Son and your big brother Jesus.

The truth of the matter is that you may still feel powerless, inadequate and insufficient to be a soldier in this type of spiritual war and to accomplish such an extraordinary defeat against a great enemy. However, when the Holy Power called "another Comforter" cometh upon you–you shall witness a power that no man on earth has ever seen before. And yes, no one really knows exactly how the Day of Judgment will really pan out, but one thing that God did reveal to me with certainty–is the PAN WILL BE IN OUR HANDS–and God will be by our sides! All vengeance belongs to God, yet God is in all of US.

Chapter Twenty-Four

The "*Kingdom Within*" Custom Sedan

Vehicle Year (Present)	Engine: New Mind
Vehicle Maker (God)	Transmission: Auto-transformation
Vehicle Model (Jesus Deluxe)	Fuel Type: Holy Spirit
Number of doors (7)	Body Type: Church of Christ
Number of cylinders (7)	Drive Type:( ) 2-wheel
Exterior color (clean)	( ) 4-wheel
Interior color (cleaner)	(√) 1-will

Mileage: 0 miles (brand new start!)

Steering: Power w/righteous handling.

Brakes: Power w/stop-sinning brakes!

Standard Accessories: Healing powers; making the blind see, lame walk, deaf hear, have whatsoever ye desire, casting out devils, displaying love, good health, good wealth, God's Favors, His Righteousness, His Blessings, and Protection etc.

WARRANTY: LIFETIME

PRICE: $ Give up your entire life of sin 100 percent.

This Is Your Down Payment and Final Payment!

(Note: If you act NOW, you can take one of these Spiritual Vehicles home today, and will cruise through life with ease!)

Chapter Twenty-Five

Jesus: The Perfect Salesman

The Father, in heaven, is in the Universal business of spiritually selling KINGDOMS. Jesus was the Father's top salesman in his Sonship! And not only was Jesus the Father's top salesman in his Sonship–he (Jesus) was the Father's First.

Pastors, ministers, and bishops are the sales reps. It is the job of the sales reps to show the new prospects (new believers) how the spiritual equipment works and how to fully navigate through the features of these spiritually powerful machines!

Therefore, the sales rep must:

1. Show you how to turn on the audio (word of God);
2. The sales reps must show you how to adjust your seats (sit with God);
3. The sales reps must show you how to buckle up and strap on the seat belt for your protection (salvation);
4. The sales reps must show you how to place the key (belief) into the ignition (faith);
5. The sales reps must show you how to start the car (get inspired);
6. The sales reps must show you how to put the car in drive (how to walk with God);
7. The sales reps must show you how to put the car in neutral (in balance with God);

8. The sales reps must show you how to avoid the reverse gear (backsliding);
9. The sales reps must show you how to accelerate its speed and tap into its full, awesome power (this is the department of prayer).

Another important feature regarding these spiritual vehicles is: **They come with no rear view mirrors!** The Father specifically excluded this particular feature from his heavenly kingdoms; as there is no need to look backwards when there are so many reasons to look, aim and go forward.

The latest, newest feature, which was just added to these righteous kingdoms of God is the *special deluxe interior packages.* Henceforth, all of God's kingdoms will be fully decorated in freshly rich Colossian "411" leather which is a very new accessory to the kingdom of God that was not made available two thousand years ago, but is available now. So, rush, order now, and get your kingdom of God vehicle immediately while such offers still last (or before the final Day of Judgment!).

Chapter Twenty-Six

Jesus: The Perfect Model

The Father (God) is Founder/Owner of these heaven-producing, spiritual machines properly known as the kingdoms of God. Jesus' purpose, here on earth, was to offer us the very awesome benefits of these very brilliant and perfectly powerful inner-machines!

Jesus was a successful businessman, in the spiritual business of selling kingdoms at the affordable price of faith. Your method of payment consists of giving up your entire life of sin. This is exactly what one of God's perfect kingdoms cost–meaning, giving up your whole life of sin. So, don't come to these heavenly counters (altars) of God, just willing to give up two or three of your best sins. **No, you have to give all of them up.**

The entire ministry of Jesus solely focused and mainly consisted of him being put on global display to show the world just how magnificent these spiritual vehicles of God actually were and are. In order to get the people to buy into God's kingdom, God needed an excellent exemplum or a perfect prototype which would serve as his "floor model". Therefore, Jesus was primed, picked, and plucked from his very birth, to do such a job.

Primarily, Jesus' mission was to prove to the world that these spiritual vehicles (kingdoms) could do everything that God said they could do. For instance, they can heal the sick; make the blind see, make the lame walk; make the deaf hear; make the stupid man become wise; make the stuttering man speak straight, cast out devils and cast away shovels. These spiritual vehicles can perform so many miraculous things. However, Jesus was the first test model of these spiritually brilliant vehicles of God.

The Bible referred to these tests as trials, tribulations, or temptations, yet, they were actually *spiritual road tests.* Jesus would never opt to miss an opportunity to display the smoothness of these spiritual vehicles when faced with catastrophic bumps in the ground (on earth). For instance, whenever Jesus would come against a bump in the ground or experience an earthly problem, he (Jesus) would automatically shift into gear and pass over it or handle it with ease. Thus, the world became in awe and would term such an episode as a miracle—however; Jesus would spiritually term it as just a display of the spiritual shock (anxiety-free) absorbent feature, which is standard with one of God's spiritual kingdoms.

Two thousand years ago, the man we know as Jesus was performing masterful, but spiritual road tests! As Jesus was, indeed, the first man to spiritually test the do-ability, durability, and divine ability of one of God's spiritual kingdoms. The people in that day did not quite understand why Jesus traveled in so many places, and in the worst places. They did not quite understand why he wanted to talk to so many people, help so many people, and heal so many people along the way. Well, Jesus was traveling to survey the land and test the terrains with one of God's vehicles on all types of surfaces (conditions). The man we know as Jesus was on a spiritual road test!

Moreover, Jesus' road test was not to confirm to the Father that his vehicles can work on earth—Jesus' road test was to prove such a point to YOU! Therefore, Jesus had to show that if a man is blind—these vehicles can heal that problem; if a man is deaf—these vehicles can heal that problem, if a man cannot walk—these vehicles can fix that problem; if a woman has *issues of blood* problems—these vehicles can cure that problem, if a person has an anxiety problem—these vehicles can curb that problem; if a person has a hatred problem—these vehicles have an answer for that problem; if a person has a jealousy-problem—these vehicles have an answer for that problem; if a person has a "look-down-on-the-poor" or "belittle-the-poor" problem—these vehicles have an answer for that problem; if a person has a low self-esteem problem (doubting disease)—these vehicles have an answer for that problem. Any problem you have, these "inner" kingdoms are created, designed and fashioned to treat and resolve it.

So, after we have seen what these vehicles can do through Jesus—the only thing the Father wants to know now is, DO YOU WANT ONE? Jesus' whole mission was to spiritually persuade you to get one. And your only way to escape God's imminent wrath on our evil world, will be for you to have one. But you must first repent because there exists one, A KINGDOM OF GOD, already in you and it is cable-ready, I mean, able-ready! Yes, it is **ABLE** and it is **READY!**

Self Mastery

How is it that you have a master's degree for something else, yet cannot master thyself?

You have been placed on earth to master this earth! Jesus mission was to show that humans could master it. We are not human beings having a spiritual experience–we are spiritual beings having a human experience. We are all spirits dressed in earthly coats and these earthly coats are known as the human flesh. The human flesh is dumb and it is very, very weak–it needs a master. God elected you to be its master.

Jesus came on this earth, as the Father's MANual instructor, to show all of us how it should be done. You will never get to heaven until you have mastered the earth: **thy flesh**. The flesh is made out of the same fabric where evil gets its fabric from–the earth. Therefore, the flesh is evil! The flesh is naturally, organically and inherently evil. The flesh is born to be wild, rambunctious, and extremely *out of order*; although it can be tamed and absolutely trained to abide by a system of rules whether good or bad, based on a person's character.

The Human Character

The human character is man's disciplinarian, designed to enforce an amenable system of rules for the flesh to obey. However, the flesh doesn't want to obey and this is why the human character, as such a disciplinarian, is truly essential.

Two thousand years ago, when Jesus embraced this earth, he had to reform the thinking and the human character of God's children, as they were severely OUT OF ORDER. Even to this day, two thousand years later, the human character is still OUT OF ORDER: To murder an innocent man for no reason means YOU'RE OUT OF ORDER. To violently rape or take sex from another human being against their will means YOU'RE OUT OF ORDER. To rob, steal, or pillage the possessions of another means YOU'RE OUT OF ORDER. To hate another person simply because of the color of their skin means YOU'RE OUT OF ORDER. To be jealous or despise a person just because they have what you do not have means YOU'RE OUT OF ORDER. To lie without any reason, or to lie with many reasons means YOU'RE OUT OF ORDER. To cheat on someone just because of the freedom to do so means YOU'RE OUT OF ORDER. To occasionally commit adultery, or periodically commit adultery or to commit adultery **every-now-and-then** or obsessively means YOU'RE OUT OF ORDER. To have concocted the world's best excuse justifying why you are committing adultery means YOU'RE OUT OF ORDER. To have sex with someone you know is married or engaged, or is in an existing-relationship—however, none of this seems to matter to you—this simply means YOU'RE OUT OF ORDER. To fornicate and have unprotected sex more times than you have protected sex means YOU'RE OUT OF ORDER. To take off work just to have sex all day means YOU'RE OUT OF ORDER. To think about sex

90% of your day, everyday means YOU'RE OUT OF ORDER. To love the touch of a man, when you too are a man; or to love the touch of another woman, when you are certainly the other woman means YOU'RE OUT OF ORDER. To be a sympathizer of the aura of the horror of the descendants of Sodom and Gomorrah means YOU'RE OUT OF ORDER. To have a conniption fit or a bad case of violent road-rage just because somebody else is driving too slowly or they may have cut in front of you means YOU'RE OUT OF ORDER. To call out sick from work when you're not sick at all means YOU'RE OUT OF ORDER. To manipulate your time cards at work just so that you can get some more money for time you didn't work means YOU'RE OUT OF ORDER. To frequently take 60-minute lunch-breaks when your lunchtime is only 30 minutes means YOU'RE OUT OF ORDER. To borrow money, clothes and other things from people yet you already know that you have no intentions on ever returning such items means YOU'RE OUT OF ORDER. To have people working for you for long hours and you know in advance that you will not be able to pay them yet you keep them sweating and working for you anyway means YOU'RE OUT OF ORDER. To love to eat again and again AND AGAIN AND AGAIN until you are so big and your weight is so unmanageably out of control means YOU'RE OUT OF ORDER. To put drugs or foreign substances into your precious body just to artificially imitate God's state of perfect peace (heaven) means YOU'RE OUT OF ORDER. To love to smoke 'til you choke, drink 'til you stink, or drink 'til you can't even **think** means YOU'RE OUT OF ORDER. When you say *I can't* more times than you say *I* *can* this means YOU'RE OUT OF ORDER. To always think negatively when there are so many reasons to think positively means YOU'RE OUT OF ORDER. To always seem to detect, locate, and find *a negative* in anything, no matter what it is means YOU'RE OUT OF ORDER. To have a seriously bad attitude-problem nine-tenths of the time, all the time means YOU'RE OUT OF ORDER. To have a very violent, anger management-problem when the matter is really not that SERIOUS at all means YOU'RE OUT OF ORDER. And when you hate to be corrected–I mean, literally hate to be corrected–when you're dead wrong and you know you're *dead wrong*–when you have an anti-corrective attitude like this–this simply means YOU'RE OUT OF ORDER. And there are hundreds of more character-traits and flaws, which time, space and opportunity will not permit me to explore more deeply. But the overall point is that we are **out-of-order!** We have to get some order in our lives by way of our characters. We are *out of order* only because we are out of control. We need some control! For, heaven is a spiritually "controlled" atmosphere! You will never get to heaven until you get some control. Heaven doesn't permit bad, uncontrollable, and unmanageable attitudes. So, get some control in your life, so that you can get some HEAVEN in your life.

The human character is definitely in need of much repair and this is really the reason why the Father almost had to rush to spiritually form Jesus–so that he may lay out the guidelines which would straighten out man's ungodly characters. Ever since the days of Adam and Eve, the world has had character-problems; and six thousand years later–GUESS WHAT? These problems still exist!

God sent to this world many prophets, messengers, and apostles just to do one thing, which was to give us a warning concerning straightening out our *sinful characters*. Your character is the only way that you can establish a relationship of salvation with God. God is not interested in you–he is only interested in your character. **Your character is the system of rules you live by.** Therefore, God is easily able to determine who you are and who your personal god is–just by reading, studying, and tracing the traits of DNA in your character. Your character is either a witness in your behalf or a suspect testifying in your disfavor. The Day of Judgment doesn't need one's hall of records–JUST BRINGETH THY CHARACTER!

God's Day of Reckoning begins and ends with the human character, as this is all the spiritual fingerprints, DNA, and evidence God will need to adjudicate Perfect Judgment. Never before have you heard the purposes and missions of God's prophets and messengers put this simply. Meaning what? Meaning, it's all in the character! As sin is the result of bad behavior and repentance is one million percent character-oriented! A person cannot repent for sins unless his or her character invokes such an action.

God is only after your character, as nothing else matters to God, except that. Your theologians have told you wrong; the entire church councils have taught you wrong. They are all wrong! Wrong answers breedeth wrong results. God would like for this planet to be abundantly abound with characters like Christ. As children of God, we must all have *Christ-like* characters. Christ means one that crushes evil. Therefore, your character must crush all your evils.

The Mind of Jesus

Jesus is a mind; he's a character; he's a personality, which is expected from the personhood of every human being. However, Jesus is not meant to be one, but a community of many. You do Jesus a disservice, when you're still expecting a man; you lend him great service, when you become such a man. Thus, *becometh* such a man; *becometh* such a woman–for, Jesus loves and needs you to complete the Father's work, here on the earth. Jesus' work consist of the same instructions he gave to Apostle Peter. Jesus told Peter: "FEED MY SHEEP!" Indeed, we have to spread the evangelism, spread the gospel; we have to spread the truth to God's people and to be good examples of such truth ourselves.

Jesus will not be a single man coming; Jesus will be a legion of men and women coming! And all these men and women will be coming in the mighty name and with the mighty name JESUS. Thus, Jesus didn't die at Calvary–Jesus transformed into a cavalry!

Jesus, this divinely powerful, worldly popular, two thousand year old figure has baffled the intelligence of the world for two millenniums running! As many people were expecting a man named Jesus, but never a MIND named Jesus! The governments of the past were expecting a man, and the governments of today are still expecting a man. The popes of the past were expecting a man, and the pope of today is still expecting a man. The priests, bishops, and pastors of the past were expecting a man, and the priests, bishops, and pastors of today are still expecting a man. The followers of the past were expecting a man, and the followers of today are still expecting a man. All these people were and still are expecting a man, yet nobody was or is expecting AN INTELLIGENT MIND by the name of Jesus. Thus, the Holy Scripture was absolutely correct that Jesus would come without observation because we are now entrusted with his occupation.

Jesus the MAN is not coming–Jesus the MIND is the only force of power, which is coming.

Jesus gave up his rights to be a MAN to divinely embrace his rights to be a PROGRAM.

The Apostle Paul said: "*Let this mind be in you, which was also in Christ Jesus*" *(Philippians 2:5).*

Jesus was a man, but now he's a mind! And he hopes that you don't mind–if he can use your mind.

The second coming of Jesus is the *second* he enters, the second he enters your spirit and the very *second* he enters your mind. Thereby, you have the SECOND COMING OF CHRIST!

Chapter Twenty-Seven

Believe In Jesus

Do you believe in Jesus?
Do you believe in Jes us?
Do you believe in Jes † us?
Do you believe in Justus?
Do you believe in just us?
Do you believe in the JUST who are US?
Do you really, honestly, and truly believe in Jesus?

Sir Jesus, the body of a seed all dressed up in a scarlet robe with stripes on his back and a crown of thorns upon his head.

Sir Jesus, a man, who held a tall, but leafy reed in his right hand, yet came back to life in *three spiritual days* as a blossomed garden of many.

Sir Jesus, God's first begotten Son who has now become a great family and population of P-L-E-N-T-Y.

Sir Jesus, they laughed at him, they mocked him, they ridiculed him as they scourged his body as it was being planted as a spiritual seed.

Sir Jesus, was not a sprout, tulip or turnip, but a divinely righteous ROSE—a brightly shining rose which *rose* in spite of the stripes and throes from crucifying foes.

WE, the people of today, are living in a very critical but crucial time in history wherein the only salvation for man, woman and child, here on this earth, is and will be to believe in JESUS.

Yet the overall purpose of the Omniscient Father is for all of his children to do both: believe and *be another Jesus*. Yes, we need more Jesus-es on this planet; we need more Jesus-es in our world; we need more Jesus-es in positions of power; we need more Jesus-es in the churches; we need more Jesus-es in the mosques; we need more Jesus-es in the synagogues; we need more Jesus-es in government; we need more Jesus-es in the court systems; we need more Jesus-es in law; we need more Jesus-es in business and finance; we need more Jesus-es in law enforcement; we need more Jesus-es teaching in elementary, high schools, and universities all over the world; we need more Jesus-es in the workforce; we need more Jesus-es helping our poor; we need more Jesus-es feeding, clothing, and sheltering our homeless; we need more Jesus-es in the family; we need more Jesus-es as friends; but more importantly, we need more Jesus-es as neighbors, i.e. international and domestic—next-door NEIGHBORS!

So, go now, **Be Another Jesus** because he is truly, certainly, and absolutely but definitely JES†US!

THIS IS: *THE JESUS SECRET!*

Afterword

Question: The book of Colossians was written by Paul and in those days, there were a lot of men who went by the name Jesus. Moreover, *Colossians 4:11*: "and Jesus which is called Justus"—is actually talking about another man name Jesus. What is your take on this?

Answer: We have to understand that names and characters in the Bible are NO COINCIDENCE—especially when Jesus is in us, lives in us and will be coming back in us! So when we read in the text: ". . . *and Jesus which is called Justus*"—this is a very powerful SIGN and not just some mere biblical coincidence:

"This is a great mystery: but I speak concerning Christ and the church."—*Ephesians 5:32.*

"But we speak the wisdom of God in a mystery, even the hidden wisdom, which God ordained before the world unto our glory."—*I* Corinthian 2:7.

"Now to him that is of power to stablish you according to my gospel, and the preaching of Jesus Christ, according to the revelation of the MYSTERY, which was kept secret since the world began."—*Romans 16:25.*

The Bible is full of mysteries. "Justus" as a name associated with Jesus had nothing to do with Paul's fellow-worker, yet everything to do with the fellowship of

Jesus Christ! These were secret codes for a latter generation:

"Even the mystery which hath been hid from ages and from generations, but now is made manifest to his saints."–*Colossians 1:26.*

You are absolutely correct–there were many men, back in those biblical times, who carried the name JESUS. But, Holy Scripture had a "special" purpose for making scripture out of this person named *Jesus "which was called Justus."* Why? It is because the 2,000 year Jesus whose name was JUSTUS had a secretly hidden meaning for The Real Jesus, whose name **IS** Jes us.

Scripture says, *"But ye have not so learned CHRIST!"– Ephesians 4:20*

And what corroborates Jesus' "NEW NAME" as Jes † us–is the abundance of Holy Scripture, which confirm that he (Jesus) is JUST US:

"Jesus Christ is **In You!**"–*II Corinthians 13: 5.*

"And by their prayer for you, which long after you for the exceeding grace of **God In You.**"–*II Corinthians 9:14.*

Jesus said: " . . . Ye shall know that I am in my Father, and ye in me, and **I in you.**"–*John 14:20.*

"That the name of our Lord Jesus Christ may be **Glorified In You**"–*II Thessalonians 1:12.*

"My little children, of whom I travail in birth again until Christ be **Formed In You.**"—*Galatians 4:19*

" . . . that the life also of Jesus might be made manifest IN OUR BODY [again through YOU]."—*II Corinthians 4:10*

" . . . By one man Jesus Christ, hath abounded unto many [ALL OF YOU!]."—*Romans 5:15*

In the earthly realm, Jesus went by the surname Immanuel, which means *God with us.* In the heavenly realm, this book proposes he (Jesus) goes by the spiritual surname *JUSTUS.* Here we have Immanuel, which means God with us. And, spiritually we have "JUST US," which means **GOD In Us!**

Lastly, if something is regarded as a mystery—the clue has to be able to bring special pieces together. If the Bible says that JESUS is a divine mystery—then the clue has to be in bringing special, biblical pieces together. If Jesus Christ is a mystery—then it's not meant to be taken literally. The Bible's purpose is NOT to reveal this mystery **"Verbatim"** but to **"Virtually Bate Him"** (reveal the mystery in clues). Therefore, JUSTUS was the clue, yet Jes † us is the answer!

Question: Theologians are calling you the master of heresy and a false prophet of heretical indoctrination! How do you respond to these blatant charges?

Answer: Even Jesus was accused of heresy! It's easy to become accused of heresy. **Heresy** simply means that you have a different view about the general belief. Yet, you don't have to agree with the general belief, when the general belief is generally wrong:

When Jesus changed the Ten Commandants to Two—that was considered **heretical!**

When Jesus was healing people on the Sabbath—that was considered **heretical!**

When Jesus nullified water-baptism and sanctified spirit-baptism—that was considered **heretical!**

When Jesus said there would be no more circumcision of the FLESH but only the circumcision of the SPIRIT—that was considered **heretical!**

To be accused of being **heretical** in the days of Jesus was considered good yet to be accused of being **heretical** in these last days is even better!

Question: Why God did not reveal the code in Jesus' name in other languages. i.e., Ιησούς: ΙΗΣΟΎΣ (Greek), Jesús; DE JESÚS (Spanish), Jésus (French), ישו, Yeshua (Hebrew/Yiddish), Isa (Arabic), Yishu (Roman), ИИСУС, БОЖЕ (Russian), JEŽÍŠ (Czech), JEZUS (Dutch) (Albanian) (Polish), ИСУС (Bulgarian), JÉZUS (Hungarian), GESÙ (Italian), İSA PEYGAMBER, HAZRETİ İSA (A.S.) (Turkish) etc.?

Answer: Jesus declared that he would rise again on *the third day*, which is biblically proven to mean three thousand years later. Therefore, had God left those

Jesus-codes in a pre-existing dialect—it would have easily been discovered and decoded a long time ago. Moreover, *The Jesus Secret* would have never survived as a mystery for 3 years—(probably not even 3 months!)—much less 3,000 yrs.

Thus, to insure the security of his secret, the Omnipotent God opted to unveil his mystery in a language that had yet to make its entry or introduction on earth.

The English language is the world's newest, baby-vernacular and the last to come in relation to all the other major languages.

Yet the English language is currently first and is the most dominant language impacting and influencing nearly all nations of the world today. Furthermore, why would God reveal a great mystery in a language that is not even popular? Would it benefit God to reveal his great mystery initially in Ibo, Basque, Xiang or Wu when over half of the people on this planet speak and understand English?

Therefore, the Most Dominant God chose the most dominant language for the initial revealing of his Greatest Mystery—The Mystery of JESUS. **This Is The Jesus Secret!**

Special Message To The Pastors

This book is not meant to bash reverends, pastors and/or bishops. Yet, it is purposely meant to bash the theologians.

For it is this religious group of scholars that is the most hateful in the eyes of God, in that, they are the ones responsible for devising the liturgies, seminary courses and theological studies that solidify the foundation for how the pastors, reverends and bishops attempt to evangelize the true gospel.

Thus, the pastors, reverends and bishops are the small fries–the spiritual **Mickey D's** in this very *unhappy* meal.

What Did Muhammad Have To Say About Jesus?

1. Was Jesus only a prophet?
Answer. For centuries, Muslims have been making the argument that Jesus was simply a prophet likened to the rest of the prophets of God. Yet Prophet Muhammad revealed that Jesus was more than just your ordinary prophet. Unlike other prophets of God, Jesus was a "**sign**" to humanity: "*And that We may make him* (Jesus) *a sign to men*"–Holy Qur'an 19:21.

2. Did Muhammad make any more references of Jesus as being more than just a prophet?
Answer. Yes! Prophet Muhammad revealed that Jesus would be an example: "*And when the son of Mary is mentioned as an example, lo! Thy people raise a clamour thereat*"–Holy Qur'an 43:57.

3. Christianity and Islam are the two greatest religions in the world. But, what is it that these two great religions do not know about Jesus?
Answer. The Bible says: "*Whereby, when ye read, ye may understand my knowledge in the mystery of Christ (Ephesians 3:4).*" The Qur'an says: "*And that We may make him* (Jesus) *a sign to men (19:21).* Yet Christians don't know "**the mystery**" and Muslims don't know "**the sign**".

4. If one wanted to make a Muslim stutter, what must one do?
Answer. Ask him or her what is the *sign* of Jesus?

5. If one wanted to make a Christian stutter, what must one do?

Answer. Ask him or her what is the *mystery* of Jesus Christ?

6. Did Jesus really die on the cross?

Answer. Jesus did not die–Jesus transformed! Yes, Jesus' flesh may have died, his human shell or seed may have died, but the spirit of Jesus still lives on:

> *"And for their saying: We have killed the Messiah, Jesus, son of Mary, the messenger of Allah, and they KILLED HIM NOT, nor did they cause his death on the cross, but he was made to appear to them as such. And certainly those who differ therein are in doubt about it. They have no knowledge about it, but only follow a conjecture, and they killed him not for certain.*
>
> *Nay, Allah exalted him in His presence. And Allah is ever Mighty, Wise.*
>
> *And there is none of the People of the Book but will believe in this before his death; and on the day of Resurrection he (Jesus) will be a witness against them"*– Holy Qur'an 4:157-159.

7. Was Jesus really healing the blind, the leprous and raising the dead?

Answer. Absolutely, according to the Holy Qur'an, it reads:

> *"O Jesus, son of Mary, remember my favour to thee and to thy mother, when I strengthened thee with the Holy Spirit; thou spokest to people in the cradle and in old age, and when I taught thee the Book and the Wisdom and the Torah and the Gospel, and when thou didst determine out of clay a thing like the form of a bird by My permission,*

then thou didst breathe into it and it became a bird by My permission; and thou didst heal the blind and the leprous by My permission; and when thou didst raise the dead by My permission (5:110)."

8. In the Bible, it makes the reference that a "day" is with the Lord as a thousand years. Does the Holy Qur'an make a similar reference?

Answer. Absolutely. In the Holy Qur'an it reads: "*And surely a day with thy Lord is as a thousand years of what you reckon (22:47).*"

9. In the Bible, Jesus is shown teaching his disciples the significant power of three days, especially *the third day.* Does the Holy Qur'an show Jesus elaborating on these three days as well?

Answer. Absolutely. In the Holy Qur'an, Jesus said: "*Peace on me the day I was born* (1st day), *and the day I die* (2nd day), *and the day I am raised to life* (3rd day!)"–19:33.

10. What does "Messiah" means?

Answer. It means *the anointed one*; one who travels, one who saves, and one who is abundantly blessed with the sword of truth.

11. Was Jesus really the Messiah?

Answer. Prophet Muhammad revealed that Jesus was indeed the true Messiah: "*O Mary, surely Allah gives thee good news with a word from Him whose name is the Messiah, Jesus, son of Mary, worthy of regard in this world and the Hereafter*"–Holy Qur'an 3:44.

12. The Bible makes specific references about the "resurrection of Jesus" but what does the Holy Qur'an have to say about Jesus' resurrection?

Answer. The Qur'an had this to say about Jesus' resurrection: "*When Allah said: O Jesus, I will cause thee to die* (physically), *and exalt thee in My presence* (spiritually), *and clear thee of those who disbelieve* (literally), *and make those who follow thee above those who disbelieve to the day of Resurrection* (for surely)"–3:54.

13. Where is heaven?

Answer. Jesus taught that God's heavenly *address* is within.

14. Did prophet Muhammad teach a similar teaching?

Answer. Indeed. In the Holy Qur'an, it reads: "*We* (Allah and His angels) *are nearer to you than your* (jugular) *life-vein*"–50:16. Well, the jugular vein of man is not outside of him–the jugular vein of man is inside of him. Allah said, "He is closer to man than his jugular vein." This all means that Allah (God) *is* in us, which corroborates the statement Jesus made: "*The kingdom of God is in you.*"

15. What about the seven heavens?

Answer. Now that we know where the "first" heaven is–it's pretty much easy to locate them all.

16. Meaning What?

Answer. For centuries, we have been taught that God had these heavenly condominiums in the sky–when actually these **condominiums** are **condoning-MEN-within!**

17. Where are these seven states, properly called heavens, mentioned in the scriptures?

Answer. The Bible refers to these seven states as the seven churches (Revelation 1:20). The Holy Qur'an refers to these seven states as the seven heavens: "*The seven heavens and the earth and those in them declare His glory. And there is not a single thing but glorifies Him with His praise, but* YOU DO NOT UNDERSTAND *their glorification*"–17:44.

18. What did the Holy Qur'an mean by: "You do not understand their glorification(s)?"

Answer. There are seven heavens within man yet God sits at the top of these seven heavens. *The seven heavens* represent the seven spiritual roads in the growth and developmental stages of man. *The earth* represents the vehicle (body) that man must navigate (control) in his spiritual journey (destiny!).

19. The Holy Qur'an makes a lot of references about the "hereafter". What is the hereafter?

Answer. The hereafter is the Garden of Bliss, which will be "**here**" but "**after**" God's Day of Judgment.

20. What is the difference between Heaven and the Garden of Bliss?

Answer. Heaven is the ultimate spiritual state in the mental and spiritual realms, whereas the Garden of Bliss is exclusively on the physical realm.

21. Is there an example of the Garden of Bliss reflected in the physical realm?

Answer. Yes there is! Read the Holy Qur'an, chapter 56 verses 28 through 34. It is there you will see the Garden of Bliss described in the physical realm as consisting of thornless lote-trees, banana trees, extensive shade, water gushing, abundant fruit and exalted couches.

Quite frankly, spiritual heaven does not have **banana trees**; it does not have bananas or trees. Spiritual heaven does not have the matter we call **water gushing**. However, the most bizarre of all is the **extensive shade** reference. How can a spiritual heaven consist of extensive shade, when shade is a reflection of physical objects or forms, of which a spirit has none?

22. Was Muhammad really a true prophet of God?

Answer. The real question is: "Who are we to say that he was not?" The Qur'an says: "*And for every nation there is a messenger (10:47).*" In the Bible, it specifically states: "*I will raise them up a prophet from among their brethren, like unto thee, and will put my words in his mouth (Deuteronomy 18:18).*"

At the time that God was preparing a prophet for the Arabs, societal conditions were miserably and terribly wretched! History records that the Arab nation went nearly three thousand years without a Divine Revelation from the Most High God. This was nearly three thousand years since the days of Moses and six hundred years after Jesus.

During this time, half the Arab population could not read or write. An abysmal apathy set in among the Arabic people, which bonded their civilization to the trenches of great incivility and immorality. This led the Arabs to such extreme and deplorable depths as barbarism, atheism, polytheism, deifying rocks and stones, marrying close relatives such as cousins and stepmothers, killing without conscience, burying their daughters alive, having wild and rampant under-aged sexual affairs, public rapes, public humiliations, public mutilations, adultery, idolatry, misogyny, chronic drunkenness, and obsessive gambling.

We should thank God that he sent the Arabs a prophet! They needed a prophet, considering that Jesus never came to them nor had any other prophet ever come to them. **Again, they needed a prophet!** If Prophet Muhammad were not the prophet to the Arabs, it would mean that this hundred million plus nation has gone over 6,000 years without a prophet or Divine Revelation communicated in their language. This would make God an unfair God–if this were true.

Therefore, it was only right that God would give them a prophet among their brethren. Was it the Arabs misfortunate that this prophet's name would be Muhammad? Would some folks feel a lot better if this prophet's name was Jack, Bill or even Frank? I'm not an Arab yet I'm not mad at God for raising them up a prophet. They desperately needed one and quite frankly–I'm glad he (God) gave them one. It makes sense that the prophet's name had to be Arabic, if he was sent to redeem Arabic people. **An English, Russian or Japanese prophet won't work for an Arabic people.**

It is truly unfair and irresponsible for any religion and/or religious people or person to assert that God only came to them. For God to give the Arabs a prophet from among their brethren is very **consistent** with the Divine Demeanor, Inimitable Impartiality and Universal Agape Love of the Most High God.

23. What would you like to say to the followers of Prophet Muhammad?

Answer. I would like to remind them that Prophet Muhammad prophesized that his TRUE followers will start experiencing a considerable **decline** post three generations after his death: "*The people of my generation are the best, then those who follow them, and then those who follow the latter.* AFTER THAT *there will come some people whose witness will go ahead of their oaths, and their oaths will go ahead of their witness*"– Narrated by Abdullah in the *Hadith* by Sahih Al-Bukhari, vol 3 book 48, Number 820.

I, further, would like to remind them that Allah revealed to Prophet Muhammad that, unlike his own followers, the followers of Jesus will be placed above those that disbelieve until the day of resurrection: "*When Allah said:* O *Jesus, I will cause thee to die and exalt thee in My presence and clear thee of those who disbelieve and make those who follow thee above those who disbelieve* TO THE DAY OF RESURRECTION–*Holy Qur'an 3:54.*"

24. So what do you suggest the followers of Muhammad to do?
Answer. The entire Muslim community must jump on Isa's (Jesus') bandwagon if they desire to be divinely carried and protected *to* the Day of Resurrection. Prophet Muhammad did a great job but it is **Isa** who is going *to take us home!*

25. Does Prophet Muhammad's Divine Revelation of the Holy Qur'an supersede the Divine Gospel of Jesus?
Answer. Prophet Muhammad said: *"And if a man believes in Jesus and then believes in me, he will get a double reward"*—Narrated by Abu Musa Al-Ash'ari in the *Hadith* by Sahih Al-Bukhari, vol 4 book 55, Number 655. In this passage of the *Hadith*, Prophet Muhammad clearly establishes a theological order of scriptural priority, which is non-existent in most Islamic societies today.

To **Believe In Jesus** is to believe in the Divine Message given to him by God: *"Then We made Our messengers to follow in their footsteps, and We made Jesus, son of Mary, to follow and We gave him the Gospel"*—Holy Qur'an 57:27.

Jesus' message is called the Gospel. The Gospel is the New Testament in the Bible. Prophet Muhammad suggested that Muslims read Jesus' Gospel, if they wanted to get the double reward. Yet, there are many Muslims who do not and others who **absolutely will not** read the Bible even if you paid them. Thereby, this makes those Muslims guilty of dishonoring the way to the double reward.

26. Are you a Christian or Muslim?
Answer. Quite frankly, I don't have a religious title–I'm simply a man of Truth! I read both the Bible and the Qur'an; and I respect both Jesus and Muhammad. I think what I am really trying to say is ...**I'm trying to get the DOUBLE REWARD!!!**

May God Bless You!

INDEX

About The Author

AIM OG is a 21st century, unorthodox spiritualist! He is a man that saddles an old song but girding what may be considered by many, a brand *New Voice.*

The man is a very galvanizing, motivational and powerful speaker yet also is that as a writer.

The literary world will immensely delight as it welcomes his uncompromisingly artistic style, savvy and simplicity in sagacities.

His analogies are almost impeccable. And his suppositions seem to be nearly as perfect as facts.

He is a man who will rapidly soar as a literary giant in today's book world. This will all come by the virtues of his giant message from a GIANT GOD within a little man named AIM OG.

He writes such truths with so much straightforwardness that it will make some people laugh, others will want to cry and the rest will be stunned, dumbfounded but dazed. Yet these are the illative side effects of what happens when one is adorned with the powerful sword of unadulterated truth.

This extraordinary man has over 20 years of theological studies, yet his most illustrative revelations all came within a span of just one year. During such time, he wrote five other fascinating books, which will enthrall the avid and prudent reader. Those books are entitled: *Be (lieve) and Behold it is!*; *Faith: An Unseen Fact*; *A Fear Not Degree Is Better Than A Ph.D*; and *Proverbs of a Man* volumes One and Two.

AIM OG is currently working on his newest, literary project. He is a freshly inspirational seed and lives in the Garden State: New Jersey.

ATTENTION!!!

This is a public announcement to all celebrities, TV personalities, actors, actresses, singers, songwriters, hip-hop lyricists, professional athletes and all other media icons. To God belongs all the well-deserved Glory for blessing you with the special gifts and/or talents that you possess. Each and every one of you is exceptional in God's eyes and has been placed, by design, in a unique situation. WITH YOUR constant contact with global cameras—you have the ability to reach millions! If you trust this book has been a blessing to you—Please Take This Vow:

During my interviews, I ___________________, promise to use man's media to help evangelize my Father's WORD by mentioning *The Jesus Secret: The Hidden Truth* as A MUST READ BOOK to all my fans, enthusiasts and people alike.

Sincerely,

Signed:_______________________

(Note) You do not have to sign your name literally—just sign it spiritually as a covenant to God.

P.S. YES, we must change the tide of secular *celebs* highly recommending the movie *Scarface,* as a MUST in every household! We are God's children, therefore, we do not advocate **death** and **drugs**—we advocate **life** and **supernatural healings**.

Send All Correspondences To:

TruBooks Publishing, LLC
c/o Aim Og
P.O. Box 234
Hillside, New Jersey
Zip 07205

Email: AIMOG@jesussecret.com

Message To God's Family

Every member of God's family must take this seed, refer to here as a book, and plant it (give it to a relative, friend or a complete stranger)—**then immediately go buy another one for oneself!**

For, God blesses those who help to evangelize his WORD. Therefore, GET your blessing from God by GIVING this one away.

"Giving is not really giving—giving is truly getting!"

May God Bless You!

Email____

Card #____

Esp.Date____________________Signature__________________________

Email____

Card #____

Esp.Date____________________Signature___________________________

Large/Bulk Orders (Paperback)

1) 25 copies of *The Jesus Secret: The Hidden Truth* @ $5.25 = $131.25.

2) 50 copies of *The Jesus Secret: The Hidden Truth* @ $5.00 = $250.00.

3) 100 copies of *The Jesus Secret: The Hidden Truth* @ $4.75 = $475.00.

4) 250 copies of *The Jesus Secret: The Hidden Truth* @ $4.50 = $1,125.00

5) 500 copies of *The Jesus Secret: The Hidden Truth* @ $4.25 = $2,125.00.

6) 1000 copies of *The Jesus Secret: The Hidden Truth* @ $4.00 = $4,000.00.

Please call our 24-hr toll free # 1-800-945-1511 for shipping and handling rates.

The Jesus Secret Series

Presents

Series of Forth Coming Books:

The Jesus Secret: Part Two!

Thy Father Which Art In Heaven by Aim Og

The Seven Heavens by Aim Og.

Prayer: The Power of The 4, 8, 12's. By Aim Og.

Proverbs of A Man volumes 1 & 2 by Aim Og.